Beyond Containers

Architecting Reliable Cloud-Native Systems with Kubernetes

Siri Chandana Chava

Preface

The early era of the cloud-native movement was defined by a singular focus: the "how." We obsessed over how to containerize an application, how to deploy a pod, and how to manage a basic cluster. In those days, Kubernetes was a tool to be mastered, a destination in its own right. Today, the landscape has fundamentally shifted. Kubernetes is no longer the goal; it is the foundation. As modern systems grow in complexity, the challenge is no longer just running containers. It is ensuring those containers form a resilient, self-healing, and truly scalable ecosystem.

This book was born out of a necessity to bridge the gap between a system that is merely "functional" and one that is "reliable." In the following pages, we move beyond basic orchestration. We explore the strategic patterns that allow platforms to thrive under immense pressure, the sophisticated automation required to eliminate human error, and the high-level architectural decisions that transform a collection of microservices into a robust production engine.

Dedication

To the engineers building the invisible systems that power our world.

Acknowledgement

I would like to express my sincere gratitude to everyone who supported and inspired me throughout the development of this book. First and foremost, I thank my family for their constant encouragement, patience, and understanding during this journey. Their support has been invaluable in helping me complete this work.

I am also deeply thankful to my mentors, colleagues, and peers whose knowledge, insights, and professional experiences have significantly enriched my understanding of cloud-native technologies and distributed systems. Their guidance and discussions have shaped many of the ideas presented in this book.

A special acknowledgment goes to the open-source community, whose innovation and collaboration continue to drive the evolution of Kubernetes and cloud-native ecosystems. The collective contributions of developers, architects, and researchers around the world have made this field dynamic and transformative.

Finally, I thank all readers, learners, and technology professionals who continue to explore, build, and innovate in the world of reliable cloud-native systems.

Contents

Chapter 1

Why Kubernetes Matters Beyond Orchestration

1.1 Architecture and Components of Kubernetes

Declarative configuration and automation are made easier with Kubernetes is an open-source, portable, and flexible platform for managing containerized workloads and services. Its ecosystem is vast and expanding quickly. Services for Kubernetes, technology, and support are easily accessible.

The word "Kubernetes" comes from a Greek word that means "pilot" or "helmsman." To get the acronym K8s, count the eight letters that divide the letters "K" and "s." In 2014, Google made the Kubernetes project publicly available. Kubernetes blends community best practices and ideas with more than 15 years of Google's experience overseeing massive production workloads. Within containers, programs can be compiled and executed. You are responsible for maintaining the containers that run the applications and making sure that the production environment never experiences any downtime. For instance, another container must start if the first one fails. If this behaviour were controlled by a system, wouldn't it make things easier?

Kubernetes comes to the rescue! Kubernetes offers a framework for the dependable operation of distributed systems. It offers deployment patterns, controls the scaling and failover of your application, and more. For instance, Kubernetes can handle a canary deployment for your system with ease.

1.1.1 Key Features and Capabilities of Kubernetes

In order to facilitate load, Kubernetes can expose a container with either its own IP address or a DNS name for balancing and service discovery. When a container has high traffic, Kubernetes can disperse network traffic and load balance it, guaranteeing a stable deployment.

- Storage orchestration Any storage system, including Kubernetes, can be used to mount public cloud and local storage automatically providers.
- **Automated rollouts and rollbacks.** Kubernetes can change the current state of your deployed containers at a predefined rate and let you specify the desired state for them. For example, you can use Kubernetes to automatically create new containers for your deployment, remove old ones, and move all of their resources to the new ones.
- **Automatic bin packing** Kubernetes can execute containerized jobs if you give it a cluster of nodes. Kubernetes is informed of the CPU and RAM specifications for every container. Kubernetes may install containers on your nodes to optimize your resource utilization.
- **Self-repair** If Kubernetes replaces the container and alerts clients until it's ready to serve if your user-defined health check fails, then terminates the container.

- **Secret and configuration management** Passwords, OAuth tokens, and SSH keys are among the sensitive data that Kubernetes can handle and keep. Without having to rebuild your container images or reveal secrets in your stack settings, you may deploy and change the application configuration and secrets.
- **Batch execution** Apart from providing services, Kubernetes can also handle your burden for continuous integration and batch processing, and if you'd want, it can replace containers that fail.
- **Horizontal scaling** either automatically based on CPU usage, using a user interface, or with a simple command scale your program up and down.
- **IPv4/IPv6 dual-stack** IPv4 and IPv6 address distribution among services and pods.
- **Designed for extensibility** Enhance your Kubernetes cluster's functionality without modifying the source code upstream.

1.1.2 Cluster Architecture of Kubernetes

Infrastructure the Kubernetes construction.

A control plane and a collection of worker computers, or nodes, make up a Kubernetes cluster. each of which executes containerized applications. For each cluster to operate Pods, at least one worker node is needed.

The worker node or nodes host the pods that make up the application workload. The control plane oversees the cluster's worker nodes and pods. In manufacturing settings, the cluster usually spans several nodes and the control plane usually spans several computers, making it highly available and fault-tolerant.

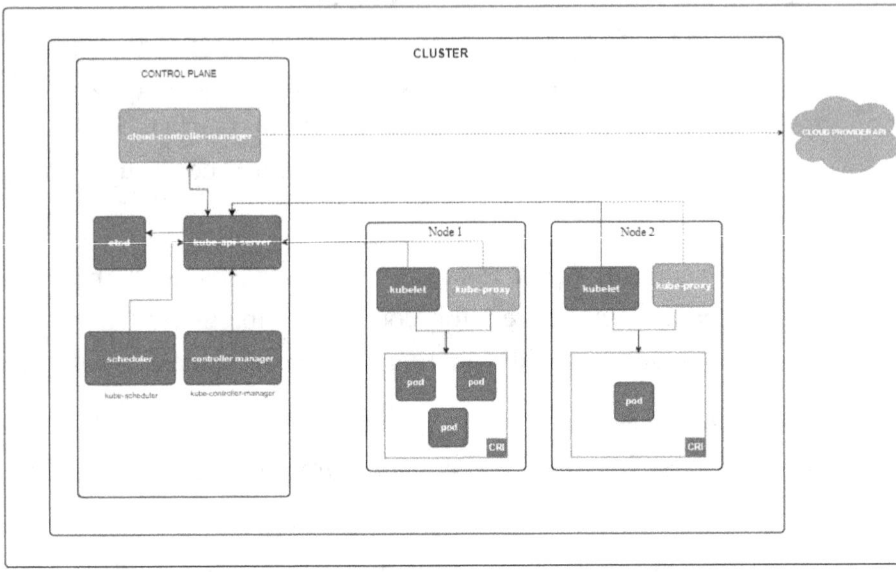

Figure 1.1: Kubernetes cluster components.

Control Plane Components

Control plane components monitor and react to cluster events, such as delivering a new pod when a deployment's replicas field is not satisfied, and make global choices about the cluster, such as scheduling. Any machine in the cluster can run components of the control plane. Instead of using user containers on this machine, setup scripts usually start all control plane components on the same system for simplicity.

1. Kube-apiserver

The Kubernetes API is made available by the API server, which is a part of the Kubernetes control plane. The Kubernetes control plane's front end is the API server.

Kube-apiserver is the primary implementation of a Kubernetes API server. Kube-apiserver may expand by adding more instances due to its horizontal scalability design. Numerous kube-apiserver instances can be launched and traffic can be divided among them.

2. Etcd

A dependable, highly available key value store serves as Kubernetes' backup repository for all cluster data. Make sure you have a backup plan for the data, etc., if your Kubernetes cluster's backing store is etc.

3. Kube-scheduler

This section of the control plane looks for newly generated pods and selects a node to run them on.

Deadlines, data locality, Standards for affinity and anti-affinity, hardware, software, and policy limitations, individual and group resource requirements, and inter-workload interference are all factors to take into account while scheduling.

4. Kube-controller-manager

portion of the control plane that manages the operations of the controller. All controllers are merged into a single binary and executed in a single process in order to simplify things, despite the fact that they are conceptually distinct processes.

There are many different types of controllers. These are a few examples of them:

- **Node controller:** Responsible for detecting and managing node failures.
- **Job controller:** It generates pods to carry out one-time tasks in place of Job objects that require completion after keeping an eye out for them
- **Endpoint Slice controller:** Establishes a link between Pods and Services by populating Endpoint Slice objects.
- **Service Account controller:** Set up new namespaces' default Service Accounts.

5. Cloud-controller-manager (optional)

Cloud-specific control logic is incorporated into a Kubernetes control plane component. By connecting your cluster to the API of your cloud provider, you may use the cloud controller manager to distinguish between components that communicate with the cloud platform and those that exclusively interface with your cluster. Only controllers unique to your cloud provider are executed by the cloud-controller-manager. The cluster does not have a cloud controller manager desktop if you are running Kubernetes on your own premises or in a classroom.

Like the kube-controller-manager, the cloud-controller-manager is a single binary that runs as a single process and includes many conceptually separate control loops. To increase performance or help with fault tolerance, you can scale horizontally (run several copies).

Node Components

Run on each node, supplying managing active pods and the Kubernetes runtime environment:

- **Kubelet**: Verifies that Pods and their containers are operational.
- **Kube-proxy** (optional): Updates the network rules for nodes. in order to implement services.
- **Container runtime**: Container-running software.

Addons

Kubernetes's functionality is expanded by addons. A few significant instances are:

- **DNS**: for DNS resolution across the cluster.
- **Web UI** (Dashboard): for web-based cluster administration.
- **Container Resource Monitoring**: For gathering and preserving container metrics

- **Cluster-level Logging**: For order to save container logs in a central log repository.

1.1.3 Objects In Kubernetes

In the Kubernetes system, permanent entities are called Kubernetes objects. These entities are used by Kubernetes to reflect your cluster's current state. Discover how to work with these objects and the Kubernetes object model.

Understanding Kubernetes objects

Permanent components of the Kubernetes system are called Kubernetes objects. These entities are used by Kubernetes to depict your cluster's current state. In particular, they are able to explain:

- Which nodes are hosting which containerized applications?
- The resources those applications have access to
- The rules governing the behaviour of those applications, including fault-tolerance, updates, and restart procedures

A "record of intent" is what a Kubernetes object is that is created and then continuously monitored by the system. In essence, you are telling the Kubernetes system the ideal workload condition for your cluster at the time of item creation.

The Kubernetes API must be used in order to create, edit, or remove Kubernetes objects. For instance, the CLI makes the required Kubernetes API calls when you use the kubectl command-line interface. Additionally, you might make use of one of the Client Libraries to directly leverage the Kubernetes API in your own projects.

Object spec and status

The object status and object specification are two embedded object-level properties that govern the setup of almost every Kubernetes object. Certain objects have specifications that you have to provide when creating the object. These specifications describe how you want the item to appear and function.

The Kubernetes system and its components supply and update the object's status, which describes its current state. In order to get each object to the intended state you specified, the Kubernetes control plane is active and continuously monitoring each object's current state.

In Kubernetes, A deployment, for instance, could be an application that utilizes your cluster. Regarding the deployment requirement, you can also specify that you want three copies of the program provided at the time of deployment. Three copies of your selected application are executed by the Kubernetes system, which then interprets the Deployment standard and adjusts the state to satisfy your needs. In the event that one of these cases fails (a status change occurs), the Kubernetes system responds to the mismatch between spec and status by resolving it , in this case by starting a new instance.

Describing a Kubernetes object

When you create an object in Kubernetes, you need to add the object spec, which outlines the item's intended state, as well as some basic information about the object, like its name. When utilizing Kubernetes to create the object API (directly or via kubectl), the information needs be supplied in the request body as JSON. Usually, kubectl receives the data in a file known as a manifest. YAML is the most used format for manifests, but JSON is also an alternative. When submitting an HTTP API request, tools like kubectl transform the data from a manifest into JSON or another supported serialization format.

1.1.4 Kubernetes security mechanisms

Kubernetes has several security features controls, APIs, and methods for defining rules that can be used to manage information security.

- **Control plane protection**

Limiting who has access to the Kubernetes API is an essential security precaution for any Kubernetes cluster.

In order to offer data encryption both Kubernetes requires you to set up and use TLS both inside the control plane and between its clients and the control plane. Moreover, data stored in the Kubernetes control plane can have encryption enabled at rest. This is not the same as encrypting data from your own workloads while it's at rest, which may also be a good idea.

- **Secrets**

Basic protection for configuration values that need to be kept secret is offered by the Secret API.

- **Workload protection**

To guarantee that Pods and their containers are properly separated, enforce Pod security standards. If you require bespoke isolation, you may also define it using Runtime Classes.

You can manage by employing network policies, you can regulate network traffic within your cluster or between pods and the external network.

To put preventative or investigative controls in place for Pods, their containers, and the images they run, you can use security controls from the larger ecosystem.

- **Admission control**

Plugins known as admission controllers intercept Kubernetes API requests and have the ability to modify or validate them depending on certain fields. When Kubernetes APIs undergo version changes, carefully crafting these controllers helps prevent unforeseen problems.

- **Auditing**

A chronological, security-relevant set of logs that display the sequence of events within a cluster is provided by Kubernetes audit logging. The cluster verifies the users' behavior, Kubernetes API-using apps, and the control plane itself.

1.2 Containerization and Microservices Architecture

A software deployment technique called containerization combines the code of an application with all the files and libraries required for it to function on any kind of infrastructure. In the past, you had to install the version of an application that matched your computer's operating system in order to use it. For instance, on a Windows computer, you had to install the software package's Windows version. In contrast, containerization allows you to build a single software package, or container, that pairs with several operating systems and hardware types.

Under an application with a microservices architecture is composed of separate components that operate as separate services. These services use lightweight APIs to communicate across a clearly defined interface. Every service has a specific purpose and is designed for commercial talents. It is possible to launch, update, and scale each service to meet the demand for particular application functions because they are separately operated.

1.2.1 Benefits of containerization

Containerization is used by developers to create and implement contemporary applications due to the following benefits.

- **Portability**

Programmers may now deploy apps in a range of scenarios without having to rewrite their code thanks to containerization. They develop a single program and distribute it across several operating systems. For instance, they use the same containers on Windows and Linux. Additionally, developers use containers to distribute updated versions of outdated application code.

- **Scalability**

Containers are efficient, low-weight software elements. For instance, because a virtual machine does not need to boot an operating system, it can launch a containerized application more quickly. As a result, software engineers can quickly set up several containers for various applications on a single system. The computing resources of the shared operating system are utilized by the container cluster, and no container hinders the functionality of other containers.

- **Fault tolerance**

Containers are used by software development teams to create error-resistant applications. To execute microservices in the cloud, they employ several containers. A single damaged container has no effect on the other containers because containerized microservices run in separate user zones. This improves the resilience and availability of the application.

- **Agility**

Applications that are containerized operate in different computer environments. Without compromising the hardware, operating system, or other application services, software engineers can debug and modify the application code. They may use the container to work on changes more quickly and shorter software release cycles.

1.2.2 Benefits of Microservices

- **Agility**

Small, autonomous teams that accept responsibility for their services are encouraged by microservices. Teams are enabled to work more autonomously and faster, and they operate inside a narrow, well-understood environment. Development cycle times are shortened as a result. Gain a lot from the total throughput of the company.

- **Flexible Scaling**

Each service can grow on its own to meet the application's demand functionality it provides thanks to microservices. Groups can now accurately determine a feature's cost thanks to this appropriately design infrastructure requirements, and sustain availability in the event that a service sees an increase in demand.

- **Easy Deployment**

Testing new ideas is made easy by microservices, which allow you to revert if anything doesn't function, which helps with continuous delivery and integration. Code changes are made easier and experimentation is permitted by the cheap cost of failure and speeds up the release of new features.

- **Technological Freedom**

A "one size fits all" strategy is not used in microservices designs. Teams are allowed to select the technology that best addresses their particular issues. As a result, teams creating microservices can choose the best tool for each job.

- **Reusable Code**

Package can be used for numerous purposes by teams when it is divided into discrete, well-defined modules. It is possible to use a service designed for one purpose as a foundation for another. Because Developers don't have to start from scratch when adding new features, this enables an application to bootstrap off of itself.

- **Resilience**

An application is more resilient to failure when it is service independent. A single component failure in a monolithic design could result in the failure of the application as a whole Microservices-based Applications reduce functionality rather than crashing when a total service failure occurs program as a whole.

1.2.3 Microservices architecture

A distributed, highly scalable modern system is made possible with a microservices design.

A submission is alienated into a number of independently deployable services that interact via APIs in a microservices architecture. This enables the autonomous deployment and scaling of each service. Large, complicated applications can be delivered quickly and frequently with this method. A microservices design, as opposed to a monolithic program, enables teams to make changes and faster addition of new features without requiring a substantial amount of rewriting of the current code.

1.2.4 Key characteristics of a microservices architecture

- **Multiple component services**

Microservices are discrete, loosely linked component services that can be developed, implemented, used, altered, and redeployed without compromising the integrity of an application or the functionality of other services. This makes it possible to quickly and simply implement each functionality of an application.

- **Highly maintainable and testable**

Microservices allow teams to evaluate new features and remove them if they prove ineffective. These speeds extending the period for new product marketing and permits code changes. Furthermore, it facilitates the identification and address errors and defects in specific services.

- **Owned by small teams**

Microservices are often developed by small, autonomous teams, which promotes the use of DevOps and agile methodologies. Development cycle times are shortened when teams are given the freedom to work autonomously and swiftly.

- **Organized around business capabilities**

Services are arranged according to business capabilities using a microservices model. Teams that work to fulfil individual functionalities are cross-functional and possess the entire spectrum of abilities needed for development.

- **Automated infrastructure**

This enables teams to independently develop and implement each service without interfering with the work of other teams. Additionally, it enables teams to launch a new service version alongside the old one.

1.2.5 Containerized Architecture

Software and dependencies can be bundled in a containerized structure, or container, that can be reliably executed in any environment thanks to the idea of a containerized architecture. Unlike the previous software deployment, where Although containers are portable, the software could not be transferred to a new environment free of errors and incompatibilities.

In a traditional virtualized architecture, containers resemble virtual machines, however they are lighter, need fewer server resources, and boot up considerably more quickly. Technically speaking, a virtual machine is a fully functional virtual operating system, whereas a container shares an operating system kernel with additional apps and containers.

Controlling and automating Containerization facilitates the software development and deployment process for operations teams and developers. Containerization has made it possible to implement "Infrastructure as code" (IaC), which entails defining the necessary deployment of infrastructure in a straightforward configuration file with as many copies as necessary. Managing microservices applications with numerous independent components is one area in which it is very helpful.

1.2.6 10 Advantages of a Containerized Architecture

Virtualization used to make it easier to distribute a single server running multiple operating systems. Dissecting operating systems and apps into software components that offer particular functionality is the main goal of containerization, is regarded as the next development of virtualization. The code becomes more effective and portable because it is divided into functions and packaged separately.

Here are ten benefits of implementing a containerized architecture:

1. **Lower costs**—on substructure operations, as a single virtual machine can host several containers.
2. **Scalability:** scaling virtual machines (VMs) or instances is not necessary at the micro-service level.
3. **Microservices** can replicate instantly thanks to deployment sets and replicas.
4. **Flexible routing**, which can be configured among services that containerization platforms inherently support.

5. **Resilience**—refreshing or redeploying with a new container from the same image is simple in the event that a container fails.
6. Complete portability across cloud environments and on-premise locations.
7. **OS independent**—running an OS is not necessary. Deploying a container engine on top of a host operating system is all that is required.
8. **Quick deployment** of fresh containers. The same environment can also be used to swiftly terminate older containers.
9. **Lightweight:** Compared to images, containers are substantially lighter and less demanding because they don't require an operating system.
10. **Faster "ready to compute"**: Compared to virtual machines (VMs), containers can be started and stopped in a matter of seconds.

1.3 Application Deployment Model Evolution

Application deployment was a challenging and unpredictable procedure before Docker. The mismatch and decreased efficiency were caused by the previous deployment techniques' reliance on virtual machines (VMs) or manual environment setup. Because of variations in dependencies, configurations, and operating systems, developers had to build code on their local system only to find that it would perform differently when pushed to testing or production systems. Debugging nightmares and a shortened software development lifecycle resulted from this problem, which is commonly referred to as "It works on my machine, but not in production".

To address some of these issues, virtual machines (VMs) were created to offer segregated application environments. However, there were drawbacks to virtual machines (VMs): they were sluggish to boot, heavyweight, requiring a whole operating system in each instance, and used a lot of memory and CPU. Organisations were unable to achieve agility during software development and deployment due to the complexity of managing and scaling virtual machines. Because of this inefficiency and unportability, Docker and containerization emerged, offering a lightweight, quick, and reliable way to package and implement software in a variety of environments.

1.3.1 Types of Deployment Strategies

Choosing a deployment method that suits the specific needs of the product is very important. There are several strategies used but let's take a look at the most widely applied ones.

1. Canary Deployment

In DevOps, canary deployment is an often-used approach. The technique, which is based on the historical practice of using canary birds by miners to detect poisonous gas for the safety of the workforce, consists of offering a new version of the software to a small group of users who are called "canaries." After that, the DevOps group watches closely the performance, stability, and user experience of the product release to unearth and troubleshoot any defects and issues before gradually rolling out the product to the entire market.

Dealing with a slightly dissatisfied user or potential technical problem, the entire methodology keeps a controlled manner and suspended rollbacks.

2. Blue-Green Deployment

This DevOps method, which is also known as "red-black deployment," actually uses two identical surroundings: the one called "Blue," which is the one that is currently live, and the one called "Green," which is the one that has the new version to be released.

This strategy allows for a smooth, critical-dimension transition, which helps in switching over the movement of people from the blue atmosphere to the green one, while the blue environment remains ready for rollback.

3. Rolling Deployment

Software deployment by this method, which is often called "phased rollout," means that the new software versions are introduced step by step across the entire system. Thus, the infrastructure can be slowly substituted with the most current software version.

Even though this deployment technique is faster than the blue-green deployment, it still complicates the reversal process more than the latter.

4. Shadow Deployment

Shadow deployment is another widely accepted deployment technique that involves running combining an application's old and new versions at the same time. In short, the DevOps team duplicates the production environment to monitor the performance of the latest application under a production-like scenario without affecting the end users.

1.3.2 How DevOps Changed the Software Deployment Landscape

The movement known as DevOps got its drive in the year 2007 and 2008 because the IT professionals were not happy with the faultiness between the software development and IT departments. DevOps came to the rescue to change conventional software development, which had long development cycles and manual transfers, and to improve the collaboration between developers and operations groups. After that, DevOps has been very progressive and has developed considerably throughout its goal of meeting the needs of digital transformation and digitization.

1. Code Integration

The integration of code in the source code repository has been automated with the use of DevOps practices such as CD/CI among others. The goal is to expedite the process of software deployment by performing testing on the code to verify its functionality and curing any faults or defects afterwards to make the software ready for release.

2. User Experience

The incorporation of DevOps into the deployment strategy also assures a good user experience. The users get the software that is tested thoroughly with the automated tests, and the monitoring, and soon the problems and issues are discovered with the aid of frequent feedback loops.

3. Security

DevOps is important for the notion of DevSecOps, which means ensuring security at every stage of software deployment while maintaining the same level of process, optimizing resources, and agility, and improving the user experience.

4. Resource Management

DevOps methodologies like Infrastructure as Code (IaC) have automatically replaced the manual infrastructure processes, which included configuring, upgrading, and maintaining, for instance, database connections, operating systems, and storage. This has resulted in the integration of code-based automated procedures, thus allowing the timely and reliable software design, testing, and deployment.

The entire process of software development and deployment has witnessed a significant transformation with the introduction of DevOps in the digital realm. Furthermore, software deployment methods have already changed and will still change for the better, safer, and faster delivery through the application of basic principles such as CD/CI (Continuous Delivery/Continuous Integration), IaC (Infrastructure as Code), Version Control System (VCS), and automation among others.

1.3.3 AI in DevOps & Software Deployment

The fusion of DevOps with AI is powerful and game-changing because both are automation heavy. The introduction of AI and machine learning to DevOps practices has led to a complete transformation. The incorporation of AI into the software development lifecycle changed teams' methods of creating, testing, deploying, and monitoring software applications completely.

Let's look at some of the most significant impacts of AI on DevOps and therefore on the software development and deployment process.

1. Data-Driven Decisions

Through the application of AI-powered analytics to enormous volumes of data, the DevOps teams get actionable insights regarding user input, business KPIs, and performance metrics. The DevOps teams then utilize the profound data-driven insights from the AI algorithm to devise collaborative and tactical plans for the continued innovation and improvement in the software development and deployment process.

2. Problem Resolution

AI-based incident management systems are a great help in creating strong IT infrastructures. The automatic recognition of issues, their instant reaction, and the finding of their root cause are among the main advantages that AI systems offer in problem solving. Furthermore, through the analysis of historical data, AI systems already have the capability to foresee where the next trouble spots might be. All this not only results in improved service for the whole system but also provides a reliable and safe environment.

3. DevSecOps

AI improves security by detecting abnormalities, automating threat identification, and reducing cyberthreats. In order to identify malicious activity and reduce the likelihood of breaches, machine learning algorithms continuously monitor and examine network data. AI can enhance threat detection and protect sensitive data by strengthening cyber defense through real-time notifications.

4. Resource and Infrastructure Management

AI helps DevOps teams use resources more effectively. AI enhances the software development and deployment processes by optimizing the utilization of cloud infrastructure and automating resource allocation depending on demands. By evaluating workload patterns and reducing downtime, AI and machine learning algorithms also enhance the scalability and administration of complex infrastructures. AI helps an organization increase its scalability, resilience, capacity, and performance by streamlining resource and infrastructure management.

1.4 Workers and Control Plane Design

Workers and Control Planes are the key components of a distributed system, like Kubernetes, with the former acting as the brain (making decisions and managing the cluster), which has a continuous feedback loop to ensure a healthy cluster, and the latter as the muscle (for example, carrying out the actual workloads of an application, such as containers/pods). Workers (Kubelet, Container Runtime) run and report back on their status after receiving instructions from the control plane (API Server, Scheduler, etc.).

An essential part of a computer network is the control plane, which controls routing—the data that travels between connected devices—and transfers information throughout the network. Network design and its supporting components are now more important than ever along with the development of computer networks as an essential component of modern business and, consequently, the global interconnectedness of people and things.

The control plane's main job is to oversee the mechanisms and procedures that decide how data flows through a network. It accomplishes this by employing routing protocols or rules that are guided by algorithms to find the best path for data to take between nodes, or devices.

1.4.1 Key terms to understanding control plane functionality

To get into the advantages of the concept of command aircraft and their functionality, it would be good to know a few words about some terms in the first place:

- **Computer network:** A computer network is made up of two or more connected electronic devices with the goal of exchanging and sending data and resources, such as routers, mobile devices, and desktop PCs, or apps. Network orchestration is the process of configuring devices and systems within a network. In order to transmit information via a physical or wireless network, networked devices addressing a network rely on communications protocols, which are rules that define how to transfer or exchange data over a network. Data routing over internet networks is made easier by a number of mechanisms, including the "Border Gateway Protocol" (BGP).
- **Software-defined networking:** A software-based network design for computer networks, "software-defined networking" (SDN) makes extensive use of interfaces for "application programming" (APIs). sets of rules that enable programs to communicate with each other, share functionality, and data.
- **Router:** Data packets are sent between networks by a router, which can be a real or virtual device. A section of routing data that has been properly structured for transmission over a network is referred to as a data packet. Physical or virtual control planes give routers the capacity to decipher data packets and choose the most efficient way to transmit them across the network. The

majority of two forward data packets, routers and control planes need sophisticated routing algorithms.

- **Switch:** One component that makes data transfer between several devices easier is a switch. Switches are essential components of contemporary computer networks, such as the Internet. The switches employ Ethernet cables to move data packets between devices and data so that users and nodes can share resources.

1.4.2 Working of control plane

Additionally, the control plane makes it easier for the modern computer networks by carrying out 4 important functions: Routing, traffic management, both load balancing and topology.

- **Routing**

One of the most important tasks that control planes perform in a computer network is routing, or figuring out the path that data will take within the network. The potential paths that information may take are contained in collections of data known as routing tables, which are essential to routing. In certain situations, the router and the control plane will consider a metric associated with each of these routes while routing the data.

To select the optimal paths, routers not only rely on their routing tables but also employ a set of guidelines or procedures. One such example is the widely used control protocol for network setup, known as "Open Shortest Path First" (OSPF). These also include the DNS is a method that converts domain names into IP addresses so that web browsers can access them.

- **Managing traffic**

The function of traffic management assigns priorities and shapes network traffic in such a way that all the devices on the network can access any application to the fullest extent, although The paths that information will follow in a network are decided by the routing process. Access control lists (ACLs) and other network restrictions that improve security and performance, are set by the administrators and enforced by the control plane. Besides, prioritizing and controlling network traffic would reduce the chances of a network or device failing.

- **Repairing network topology**

The control plane maintains the network topology, which is usually displayed as a network graph that illustrates the arrangement of computers and other devices, in addition to controlling and guiding network traffic. The latter is a difficult effort that is accomplished by the computer working in tandem with physical hardware elements such as routers and programs. The control plane keeps the network under control by keeping up with specific routing tables that supply the data topology transfer instructions over a network for the most efficient outcome.

- **Load balancing**

Load balancing is a method that involves effectively dividing network traffic between several servers, which affects user experience and system availability improvement are the main advantages. The operation is performed at the control plane. The load balancing, along with the control planes facilitating it, is a fundamental aspect of the functionality of most of the popular websites and applications that get millions of user requests daily. The scheduler is an algorithm that assigns tasks to control plane nodes while trying to achieve the highest utilization of computing resources.

- **High availability and Clustering**

Keeping data flowing across network nodes is crucial for the control plane to preserve a balance between workflow and traffic. Clustering, which is the process of combining a group of computers so that their skills can be pooled to produce a single functional entity, is usually included in this. Both internal and external traffic, or data that comes from within a network and data that comes from outside, can be balanced using "control plane load balancing" (CPLB) outside of it—allows the control plane to have high availability outside of it, respectively.

1.4.3 Kubernetes Worker

One essential part of a Kubernetes cluster that is in charge of executing containerized apps is a Kubernetes worker, also known as a worker node. The following lists the main functions and parts of a Kubernetes worker node:

- **Node:** Kubernetes schedules and executes your application workloads on the worker node, which might be a machine, either real or virtual. Every node in the cluster has the services needed to run the smallest deployable computing units are called pods, and they Kubernetes allows for creation and control.
- **Kubelet:** This agent executes on each worker node to ensure that containers are operating within a pod. The Kubelet confirms the functionality and health of the containers listed in a collection of PodSpecs, which are usually provided by the master node.
- **Container Runtime:** Running containers is the responsibility of this software. Docker, containered, and CRI-O are just a few of the container runtimes that Kubernetes supports.
- **Kube-proxy:** On every worker node, it acts as a system deputation, managing the network rules on those nodes. Your Pods can communicate over the network from network sessions thanks to the network rules that are located within or outside of your cluster.

1.5 Difficulties in Large-Scale Kubernetes Environments

An open-source technology called Kubernetes may automate containerized applications' deployment, scalability, and upkeep as a container orchestration system. Nevertheless, a variety of problems related to the management of Kubernetes clusters have arisen because of their large-scale operations and need to be solved in order to guarantee these operations' dependability and effectiveness.

1.5.1 Challenges in Managing Kubernetes Clusters at Scale

1. **Difficulty and Learning Process:** Kubernetes belongs to the cutting-edge technologies that are hard and one needs to go through a steep learning curve to get a grasp of it. The difficulties in resource management get multiplied by the number of clusters and nodes. Such a scenario could lead to the situation where it was difficult to keep the clusters consistent and to make sure all the team members were informed about the system.
2. **Interoperability Issues:** The differences in Kubernetes clusters and their environments could turn out to be the biggest problem. The apps in various contexts and clusters must interact with each other effectively, which can be considered as a critical factor. This could also mean that there will be a control that most probably will not be manageable over a vast number of clouds, clusters, users, and policies.
3. **Scaling and Resource management:** It is a matter of great importance to scale a Kubernetes cluster to solve the problem of rising demand. Resource management takes more effort to get the performance as the number of applications and nodes gets larger. This means that the infrastructure will have to be able to handle the load without having any server outages or downtime.

4. **Security and Access Control:** One of the problems arising with the increase in the number of Kubernetes clusters is security. Access control and the handling of security issues must be done properly for this security problem to be eliminated. This means that Role-based Access Control (RBAC) must be put into practice, and user rights must be administered in a right way.
5. **Maintenance and Upgrades:** With the growth of the number of clusters and nodes, the maintenance burden is also increased. It is more challenging and time-consuming to follow standard procedures such as making a list of the deployed applications, connecting the clusters, and carrying out upgrades.

1.5.2 Solutions for Managing Kubernetes Clusters at Scale

1. **Standardization and Consistency**

The management of Kubernetes clusters can only be effective if there is standardization and consistency. All this means is to use the same tools and procedures when deploying workloads, creating clusters, and modifying existing components. The process of maintaining consistency aids in the quick identification of errors and the prompt restoration of the cluster to its desired state (CODE -1).

2. **Automated Scaling**

Properly managing Kubernetes clusters in a big way necessitates the use of auto-scaling systems. The infrastructure can take care of the demand without having any server outages or downtime through the help of techniques like, for instance, "Horizontal Pod Autoscaler" (HPA), which is capable of automatically scaling resources in accordance with the demand (code-2).

Platform engineering is the process of developing a standardized platform for the deployment and management of applications. Amongst the benefits of this are the easier handling of multiple Kubernetes clusters in different settings through the use of tools like Red Hat Advanced Cluster Management.

3. Holistic Management Approach

A comprehensive management strategy takes into account every facet of managing a Kubernetes cluster, such as resource management, security, and access control. This entails recording all processes and making sure that everyone involved understands their roles and responsibilities.

4. Use of Tools and Methodologies

It is necessary to use suitable tools and methods when managing Kubernetes clusters on a large scale. This includes adopting techniques such as GitOps for managing infrastructure as code and also utilizing tools such as Kubernetes Dashboard for cluster monitoring and management.

1.5.3 How does Kubernetes benefits in organizations

Applications in containers are managed, automated, and scaled with Kubernetes, a container orchestration platform that is open-source.

Organisations may now more easily develop and deploy applications across various cloud environments without worrying about software incompatibilities or functional conflicts thanks to containerized microservices. According to the CNCF 2022 Annual Survey, around 80% of organisations now use container technology for production applications due to its simplicity of deployment. However, the demand for more efficient management of these widely dispersed settings at scale has increased along with the adoption of containers.

Teams are using container orchestration tools like Kubernetes to handle this complexity. The platform's goal is to assist DevOps teams in optimizing the distribution of computational resources among all containerized workloads during deployment.

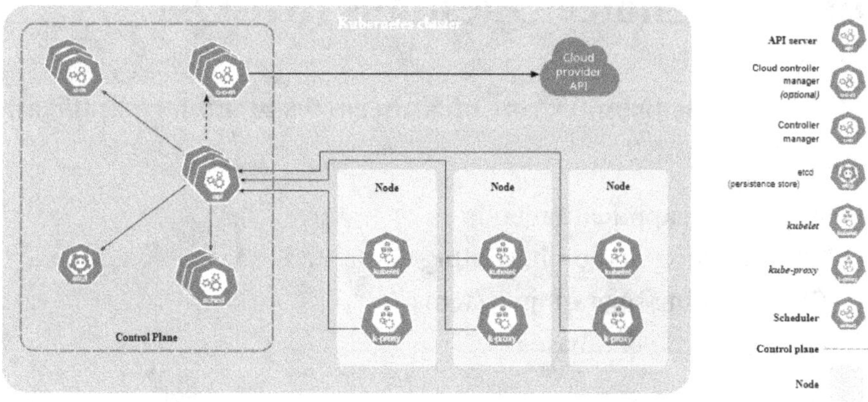

Figure 1.2: Kubernetes Cluster Components

While a handful of these solutions exist, Kubernetes has become the de facto industry standard, offering the following benefits:

- **Container deployment.** Container orchestration platforms automate daily operations for processes such as the re-creation of failed containers and rolling deployments. This helps to avoid downtime for end users.
- **Automated scaling.** Due to expansion via satisfactory constitution regarding resource assiduousness, Kubernetes is adequate to scale the applications and services subject to rank.
- **Self-healing.** Not only does the system take care of node failures and rescheduling of sick pods, but it also does the restarting, replacing, or terminating of failed containers automatically. This important part reduces the necessity of human interference and supports the availability of the system.
- **Extensibility and technology ecosystem.** Kubernetes is a free software that has a large, active and growing community of developers, plug-ins, extensions, and technologies to increase its functionality. By making the platform more versatile through different use cases, teams can adapt it, according to their specific needs.

Multiple-Choice Questions (MCQs)

1. **What is the primary role of Kubernetes in modern application environments?**

   A) Writing application code
   B) Managing and orchestrating containerized workloads
   C) Replacing operating systems
   D) Designing databases

2. **Which of the following is a core component of the Kubernetes control plane?**

   A) kubelet
   B) kube-proxy
   C) API Server
   D) Container runtime

3. **In Kubernetes, worker nodes are mainly responsible for:**

   A) Storing cluster configuration only
   B) Running application containers and workloads
   C) Managing DNS records externally
   D) Replacing the control plane

4. **What is a major advantage of containerization in microservices architecture?**

   A) It makes applications dependent on one environment
   B) It allows each service to run independently and consistently
   C) It removes the need for networking
   D) It eliminates all security issues

5. **Which deployment model came before containerized and cloud-native application deployment?**

   A) Serverless deployment
   B) Virtual machine and monolithic deployment

C) Edge-native deployment
D) Kubernetes-native deployment

6. **Which Kubernetes component runs on each worker node and communicates with the control plane?**

A) etcd
B) kubelet
C) Scheduler
D) Controller Manager

7. **Why is Kubernetes considered “beyond orchestration”?**

A) Because it only schedules containers
B) Because it also supports scalability, resilience, service discovery, and self-healing
C) Because it replaces all programming languages
D) Because it is only used for small applications

8. **Which of the following is a challenge in large-scale Kubernetes environments?**

A) Simplified networking with zero complexity
B) Easy management of all clusters without monitoring
C) Increased operational complexity and resource management
D) Elimination of infrastructure costs

9. **What is the function of the Kubernetes Scheduler?**

A) It stores cluster state
B) It decides which node should run a pod
C) It builds container images
D) It writes YAML files automatically

10. **How does Kubernetes support application reliability?**

A) By manually restarting failed applications
B) By removing all node failures
C) By automatically managing failed containers and desired state
D) By preventing all software bugs

Answer

1	2	3	4	5	6	7	8	9	10
B	C	B	B	B	B	B	C	B	C

Chapter 2

Designing For Reliability And Resilience

2.1 Multi-Cluster and Multi-node Architectures

Multi-cluster Kubernetes is the administration of multiple Kubernetes clusters a collection of nodes working with one another to coordinate and execute containerized applications. These clusters may be spread across different data centers, geographical locations or cloud providers to ensure high availability, fault tolerance and better performance.

Multi-node architecture A server design is a system design that integrates multiple individual computer systems onto a single chassis. Through the use of common infrastructure such as power, cooling, and management systems, each node is a stand-alone server capable of operating its own operating system and workloads.

This architecture proves to be especially useful in an environment where space, scalability and energy efficiency are of concern to us. Common uses cases include high-performance computing (HPC), hyperscale servers, cloud-native applications, and edge deployments where it is profitable to run multiple servers in a smaller physical footprint.

A multi-node architecture takes a number of computing nodes and pulls them into a common chassis with each having its own CPU, memory, storage and networking. The centralized components that are present in the server cabinet include high-efficiency fans, a redundant power supply, and a backplane for network connectivity. This reduces both the total power use and physical size and allows each node to operate autonomously and exploit the shared infrastructure.

Most systems have or can have remote management, either by node or centrally, using interfaces such as IPMI or Redfish. This enables administrators to provide firmware updates, distribute workloads among nodes and monitor health conditions. In HPC or AI training clusters, closely coupled parallel workloads are supported via high-speed interconnects, including PCIe Gen5 or InfiniBand, which are frequently utilized to link nodes with minimal latency.

Applications that need scale-out performance, such as distributed databases, cloud-native workloads, and containerized microservices, are best suited for a multi-node server. Systems built using this architecture combine several separate nodes into a common chassis. This method is frequently used in data centers to optimize cooling efficiency through common thermal zones, simplify management, and simplify cabling.

2.1.1 Advantages of Multi-Cluster Kubernetes

For businesses that must oversee intricate infrastructure and applications, using multi-cluster Kubernetes offers a number of advantages. The primary benefits are as follows:

- **Flexibility**

Organizations can deploy their apps across many environments, including private clouds, on-premises data centers, and numerous public cloud providers, by using multi-cluster Kubernetes. This freedom allows businesses to choose the finest infrastructure and services for their unique requirements and lessens vendor lock-in.

- **Availability, Scalability, and Resource Utilization**

By distributing workloads across multiple Kubernetes clusters, you can provide increased availability and redundancy and reduce the susceptibility to a single point of failure. Scheduling Workloads may continue to run on other clusters in case one of them fails. Also, through the distribution of the load in different data centers or regions, as well as the addition of additional resources, multi-cluster Kubernetes helps to scale your applications.

Multi-cluster Kubernetes can distribute workloads to multiple clusters and can optimize the use of resources. This will ensure that it performs optimally and will prevent overuse of resources by a single cluster. You can also better allocate resources based on the specific needs of each service by grouping specific services or components in separate groups.

- **Workload Isolation**

In multi-cluster Kubernetes, you can separate different workloads, such as development, staging and production environments, to different clusters. This reduces cascading failures and fault tolerance. Also, workload isolation can be an option to provide strict resource limits and security policies per cluster.

- **Security and Compliance**

By establishing clusters in different countries or states, you can comply with the standards of data sovereignty and legal requirements. This ensures that the data is handled and it is stored within the boundaries of a district. In order to grant even greater security to your infrastructure and apps, multi-cluster Kubernetes allows you to impose more specific security policies and access controls on each cluster.

2.1.2 Challenges of Multi-Cluster Kubernetes

Despite all the advantages of multi-cluster Kubernetes, a number of challenges are faced in the management and running of multiple clusters that are taken care of by organizations. Among the main obstacles are:

- **Configuration and management complexity**

Maintaining uniform settings, resource definitions, and deployment manifests across all clusters is necessary for managing several clusters. This may make configuration management more difficult and raise the possibility of configuration drift or cluster discrepancies.

- **Network connectivity and latency**

Network connectivity and latency might become crucial concerns as workloads and services are dispersed among multiple clusters, possibly in different geographic regions. It can be difficult to minimize latency while maintaining safe and dependable communication between services in various clusters.

- **Cross-cluster service discovery and load balancing**

Services in a multi-cluster environment must find and connect with other services in other clusters. Compared to a single-cluster configuration, implementing load balancing and service discovery across clusters can be more difficult.

- **Monitoring and observability**

Organisations must compile and correlate metrics, logs, and traces from every cluster to provide a comprehensive picture of the system's health and performance, which makes monitoring many clusters difficult. To do this, multi-cluster data management, centralized monitoring and observability systems must be put in place.

☛ Security and access control

Managing credentials, access restrictions, and security policies is more difficult when there are several clusters. It takes careful planning and execution to guarantee uniform security configurations and policies across clusters while reducing the explosion radius in the event of a security problem.

☛ Multi-node architecture

Hosts, nodes, a shared file system, and a load balancer form the foundation of the Transfer CFT multi-node architecture. Every node is seen as a single Transfer CFT instance, regardless of how many servers are supporting the nodes from outside the cluster.

The multi-node configuration consists of:

Multiple nodes can access the same files using the same configuration when using a shared file system (infrastructure). Data flows, partners, internal data files, communication, configuration, and application transferable files are all made possible by the shared disc.

A hardware or software load balancer (infrastructure) that allows incoming connections to go through. The incoming traffic is distributed among the many hosts by the load balancer. Nevertheless, the load balancer is not used by the outgoing traffic.

Each host has a connection dispatcher (Copilot component) that sends connections to nodes running on the same host after checking the host for incoming connections. For z/OS platforms, refer to VIPA load balancing in the Transfer CFT z/OS Installation and Operation Guide.

One node manager per host (Copilot component), which observes every node. The node manager takes into account the activity of other node managers while determining whether to restart a node that goes down. The file system lock manager's locks serve as the foundation for the monitoring system or the resource lock manager. Additionally, the node manager has its own watchdog that is used to prevent incorrect behavior after a shared file system auto-unlock, for instance, due to NFSv4 lease time. If the watchdog does not receive a keep-alive from the node manager, all local nodes are killed, and a relock is requested.

One synchronous communication media dispatcher per host (Copilot component), which allows the use of the media feature for synchronous communication in a multi-node setting.

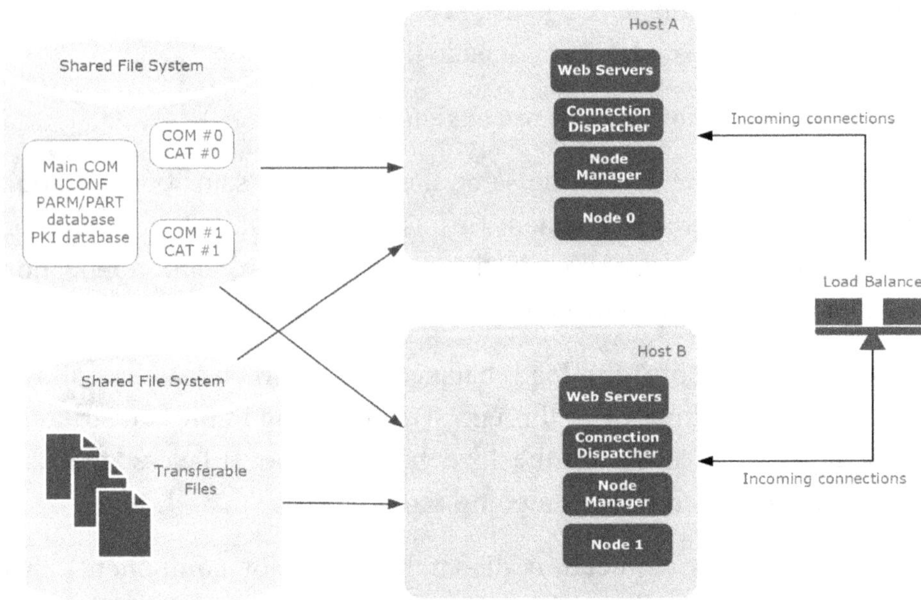

Figure 2.1: Normal Functioning of Multi-node

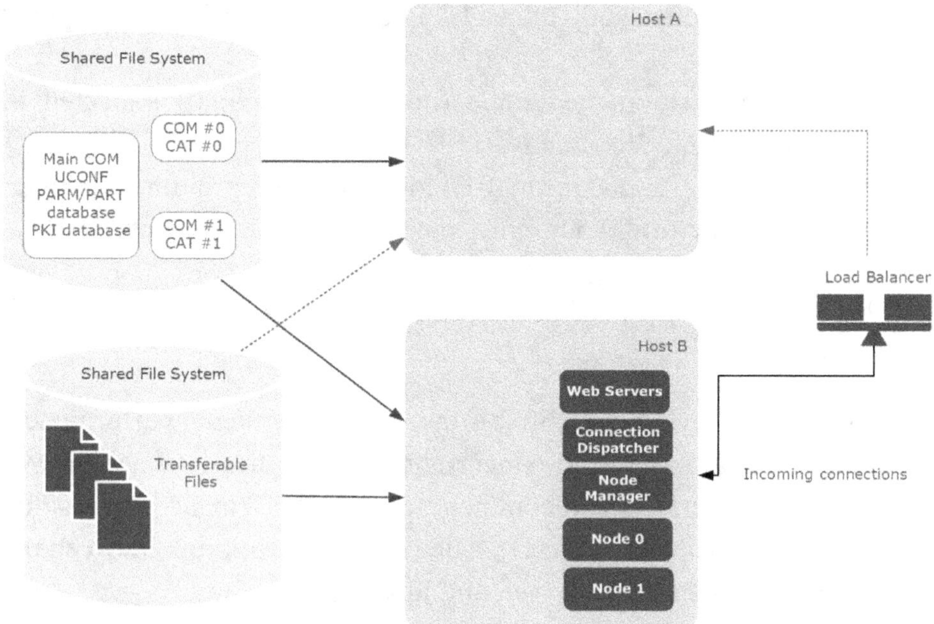

Figure 2.2: If Host A goes down, then Host B takes over Node 1

Runtime files

A shared file system contains all of the runtime data.

Nodes share the internal data files listed below:

- Parameter internal data files (CFTPARM)
- Partners' internal data files (CFTPART)
- Unified configuration (UCONF)
- PKI base (CFTPKU)
- Main communication media file (CFTCOM)

The following internal data files are node-specific, and the filename is flagged by the node identifier:

- Catalog (cftcata00, cftcata01,) located in <cft_runtime_dir>/data
- Communication media file (cftcom00, cftcom01,) located in <cft_runtime_dir>/data
- Log files (cftlog00, cftlog01,) located in <cft_runtime_dir>/log
- Output file (cft00.out, cft01.out,) located in <cft_runtime_dir>/run
- Account file (cftaccnt00, cftaccnt01,) located in <cft_runtime_dir>/accnt

Caution: Transfer CFT is sensitive to the shared file system's performance, as transfer requests perform concurrent access to the database (COM, catalog, parameters). We recommend a high-performance shared file system, a solid-state drive (SSD), a dedicated network link between the clients and the file system server, and low latency < 2ms.

2.2 Horizontal and Vertical Scaling Mechanisms

With powerful features to optimize resource utilization and cut expenses, Kubernetes provides the best platform for orchestrating containerized applications. Autoscaling, a method that guarantees operating efficiency and generates substantial cost savings, is a crucial participant in this optimization game.

Increasing cacmore servers or instances is known as horizontal scaling.

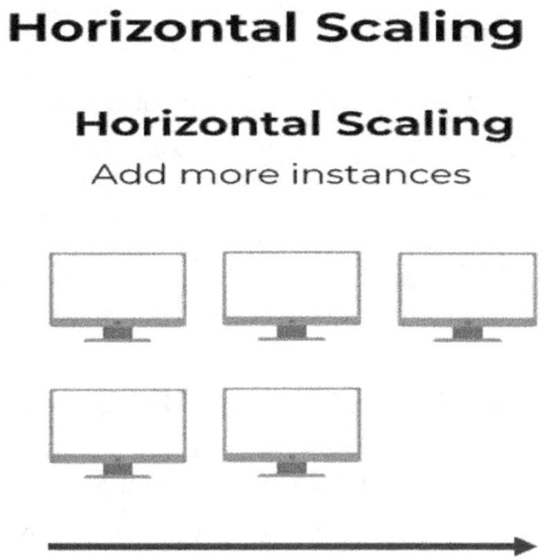

Figure 2.3: Horizontal Scaling

Increasing a single server's resources (CPU, RAM, etc.) to meet increased demand is known as vertical scaling.

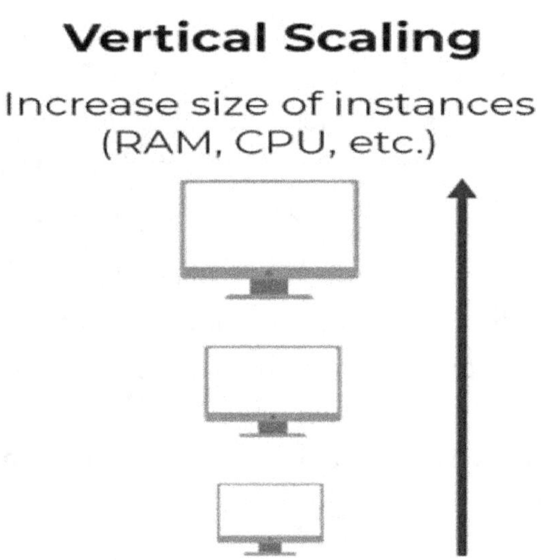

Figure 2.4: Vertical Scaling

Kubernetes Autoscaling: The Basics of Horizontal and Vertical Scaling

In an attempt to reduce unnecessary expenditure, Kubernetes autoscaling is based on the intelligent allocation of resources to the actual demand. Alongside the four primary Kubernetes autoscaling solutions: Karpenter, Cluster Autoscalers, Vertical and Horizontal Pods, it is time to discuss the differences between the different methods of scaling.

2.2.1 Horizontal Pod Autoscaling

A Horizontal Pod Autoscaler in Kubernetes attempts to automatically scale the workload to meet demand by updating a workload resource (such a Deployment or Stateful Set).

Horizontal scaling is the process of deploying additional pods in response to an increase in load. This is not the same as vertical scaling, which in Kubernetes would include giving the task's running pods greater resources (such memory or CPU).

The Horizontal Pod Autoscaler tells the workload resource (the Deployment, Stateful Set, or other comparable resource) to scale back down if the load drops and there are more Pods than the designated minimum. Autoscaling of the horizontal pod has no effect on objects that cannot be scaled, such as a DaemonSet.

One resource and controller for the Kubernetes API is the Horizontal Pod Autoscaler. The resource dictates how the controller acts. Operating inside the Kubernetes control plane, the horizontal pod autoscaling controller regularly modifies the target's (like a deployment) intended scale to meet observed criteria like average CPU or memory consumption or any other custom measure you supply.

How does a Horizontal Pod Autoscaler work?

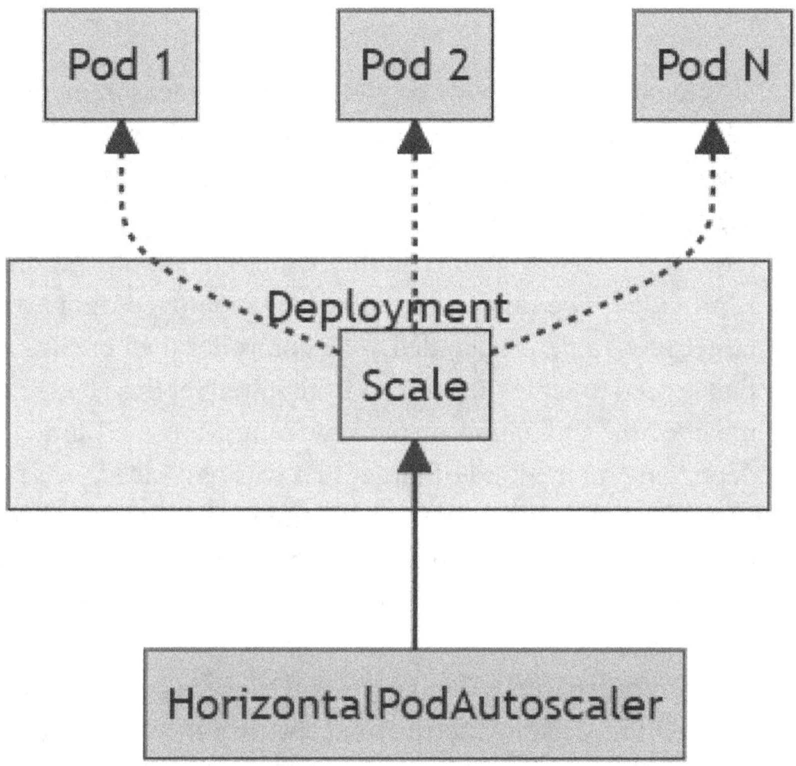

Figure 2.5: Horizontal Pod Autoscaler controls the scale of a Deployment and its Replica Set

Horizontal pod autoscaling is not a continuous process; rather, it is implemented by Kubernetes as an intermittent control loop. The kube-controller-manager's --horizontal-pod-autoscaler-sync-period setting determines the interval, which is 15 seconds by default.

The controller manager compares resource usage to the metrics listed in each Horizontal Pod Autoscaler definition at each cycle. After locating the target resource provided by the scale TargetRef, the controller manager chooses the pods using the target resources. spec. selector labels. The metrics are then obtained from either the custom metrics API (for all measures) or the resource metrics API (for per-pod resource metrics).

- The controller retrieves per-pod resource measurements (such CPU) from the resource metrics API for every Pod that the Horizontal Pod Autoscaler targets. The controller determines the utilization value as a percentage of the pertinent resource request for each container in the pod if a target utilization value is provided. The raw metric values are employed right away if a target raw value is specified. The controller then creates a ratio that is used to scale the number of required replicas by taking the mean of the utilization or the raw value across all target Pods, depending on the kind of target that was provided.
- Please be aware that CPU utilization for the Pod won't be defined, and if some of the containers in the Pod don't have the proper resource request set, the autoscaler won't do anything for that metric.
- The controller works similarly to metrics for per-pod resources. for per-pod custom metrics, except that it makes use of raw numbers rather than utilization values.
- A single measure that characterizes the object in question is retrieved for both external and object metrics. The ratio shown above is the result of comparing this statistic to the goal value. This amount can be split by the number of pods if desired in the autoscaling/v2 API version prior to the comparison.

2.2.2 Vertical Pod Autoscaling

In order to automatically change infrastructure resource requests and restrictions to reflect actual consumption, a Vertical Pod Autoscaler in Kubernetes modifies a workload management resource (such a Stateful Set or Deployment).

Allocating more resources (such CPU or RAM) to the active pods in order to achieve vertical scalability task in response to an increase in resource demand. This is sometimes referred to as autopilot or rightsizing. This is not the same as horizontal scaling, which would require more Pods to be deployed in order to disperse the load across Kubernetes.

In order to avoid resource waste, if resource utilization decreases and Pod resource requirements beyond optimal levels, the Vertical Pod Autoscaler notifies the workload resource (the Stateful Set, Deployment, or other comparable resource needs) to retreat.

The Vertical Pod Autoscaler is implemented as a controller and a resource in the Kubernetes API. The controller's actions are determined by the resource. Operating in the Kubernetes data plane, the vertical pod autoscaling controller periodically modifies the resource demands and limitations of its target (such as a deployment) in response to real-time events like out-of-memory (OOM) issues, historical resource utilization, and cluster resource availability.

How does a Vertical Pod Autoscaler work?

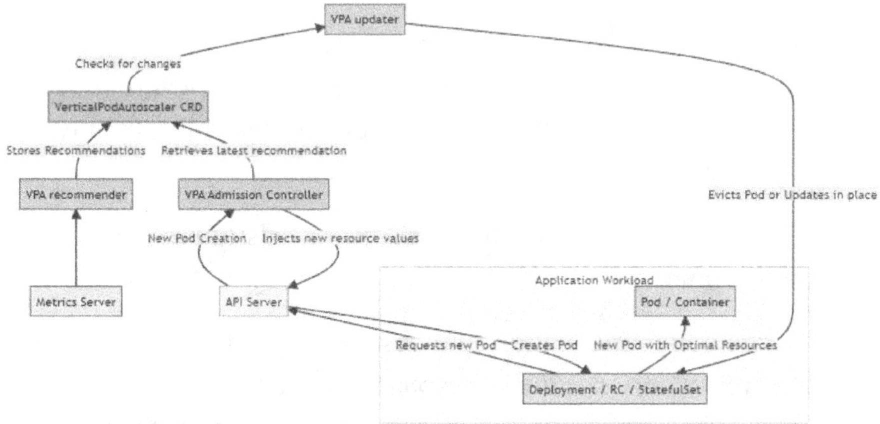

Figure 2.6: Vertical Pod Autoscaler controls the resource requests and limits of Pods in a Deployment

Vertical pod autoscaling is implemented by Kubernetes using a number of cooperative components that operate sporadically; it is not a continuous operation. There are three primary parts to the VPA:

- The recommender, which makes suggestions after analyzing resource utilization.
- By removing pods or altering those already in place, the updater responds to Pod resource demands.
- Additionally, the webhook for Resource suggestions are applied to freshly created or remade pods by the VPA admission controller.

Once per period, the Recommender checks the resource usage for each of the targeted Pods of each Vertical Pod Autoscaler specification. In order to analyze the actual CPU and memory consumption, the Recommender obtains the metrics from the resource metrics API, locates the target resource denoted by the targetRef, and chooses the pods using the target resources. spec. selector labels.

For every Pod that the Vertical Pod Autoscaler targets, the Recommender examines both recent and historical CPU and memory consumption data. It looks at:

- Examine past consumption trends over time.
- Variability and peak usage to provide enough headroom
- Out-of-memory (OOM) issues and other mishaps involving resources

The Recommender generates three different kinds of recommendations based on this analysis:

- Target recommendation (the best resources for normal use)
- Lower bound (minimum resources that are viable)
- Upper limitation (maximum resources that are reasonable). The status. The recommendation field of the Vertical Pod Autoscaler resource contains these suggestions.

The updater component keeps an eye on the Vertical Pod Autoscaler resources and contrasts the suggestions with the existing Pod resource requests. If the update policy permits it and the discrepancy beyond predetermined criteria, the updater has two options:

- Evict Pods, causing them to be recreated using fresh resource requests (conventional method)
- When in-place Pod resource modifications are allowed by the cluster, the updated pod resources remain in place without being evicted.

The cluster capabilities, the set update mode, and the kind of resource change required all influence the technique that is used. When available, in-place updates prevent Pod disturbance; however, the resources that can be changed may be restricted. To reduce the impact on services, the updater honors Pod Disruption Budgets.

Pod creation requests are intercepted by the admission controller, which functions as a modifying webhook. Before the Pod is built, it determines whether a Vertical Pod Autoscaler is targeting it Then, if applicable, implements the recommended resource requirements and limitations. More specifically, the Target proposal from the Vertical Pod Autoscaler resources status recommended stanza is used by the admission controller to request the new resource. Whether brand-new pods are produced during initial deployment, following an updater eviction, or as a result of scaling activities, the admission controller makes sure they begin with resource allocations that are suitably scaled.

2.2.3 Best Practices for Kubernetes Auto-Scaling

- **Monitor and Analyze:** Keep a close eye on the performance metrics, user traffic patterns, and resource usage of your application. You can use this information to make well-informed choices regarding resource allocation and scaling thresholds.
- **Set Appropriate Scaling Metrics:** Depending on the needs

and features of your application, select the appropriate scaling metrics (CPU, memory, or custom). Get the best possible balance between resource responsiveness and efficiency by trying and adjusting.

- **Evaluate and Validate:** Vigorously experiment with auto-scaling policies on development or staging environments before deploying them into production. You need to test your scaling setups to ensure that they operate as desired by simulating different traffic conditions.
- **Start Conservatively:** When you are more confident in the performance and scalability of your application, you can begin with more conservative scaling settings and ramp up thresholds. Avoid aggressive scaling policies which might lead to instability or unnecessary consumption of resources.

2.2.4 The advantages of Kubernetes Auto-Scaling.

- **Optimized Application Performance:** Auto-scaling ensures your apps get the resources they need to ensure they perform optimally, regardless of the workload. It has a fast response time and does not fall in performance in times of traffic intuition.
- **Cost Optimization:** Auto-scaling means that you only pay what you need at one point at a certain time. The use of resources can be optimized to reduce costs and avoid unnecessary over-provisioning by Adapting to demand by scaling up and down.
- **Enhanced Fault Tolerance:** Auto-scaling enhances fault tolerance because it separates the work load by a number of pods. Kubernetes has the capacity to immediately spin up extra replicas in the case that a pod malfunctions or stops responding, preserving service availability and avoiding downtime.
- **Simplified Management:** By automating the process, Kubernetes abstracts away the difficulty of scalability. Scaling

policies can be specified, and the platform will take care of the rest. This lowers operating overhead and allows your team to concentrate on other important duties.

2.3 Strategy of resource management and scheduling

The amount of each resource that a container requires can be optionally specified when defining a Pod. Although there are additional resources, CPU and memory (RAM) are the most often specified.

The kube- The scheduler determines which node to put the Pod on based on the resource request you make for the containers in the pod. The kubelet ensures that the operating container doesn't utilize more resources than you have specified when you establish a resource limit for a container. Additionally, the kubelet sets aside a minimum of the designated quantity of that system resource for the use of that container.

It's difficult to guarantee productive work on a project; you must allocate resources appropriately so that they are as productive as possible and not overworked. Project managers must also guarantee that the project will be completed on schedule and within the allocated budget. Project managers occasionally employ resource scheduling to satisfy all of these demands.

Key takeaways:

- Resource scheduling is a part of project resource management that aims to sequence project tasks in line with resource availability.
- The advantages of doing this are removal of bottlenecks and increased productivity.

- To schedule resources the right way, you need to audit your resources and demand for them, set priorities, and simulate resource allocation scenarios to find an optimal resource schedule.

2.3.1 Requests and limits

It is feasible (and permitted) for a container to utilise more resources than what is specified in its resource request if the node hosting the Pod has a enough supply of that resource.

For instance, a container may attempt to utilise more RAM if You set a memory request of 256 MiB for it, and it is in a pod scheduled to a node with 8GiB of memory and no other pods it.

Limits are another matter. The kubelet (and container runtime) applies the CPU and RAM limitations, which are then finally enforced by the kernel. The Linux kernel uses cgroups to impose limitations on Linux nodes. Enforcement of CPU and memory limits behaves somewhat differently.

CPU throttling enforces CPU restrictions. When it approaches that limit, the kernel will restrict access to the CPU that matches the container's limit. Therefore, a CPU limit is a hard limit that the kernel imposes. It is not permitted for containers to use more CPU than their CPU limit allows.

The kernel uses out-of-memory (OOM) kills to enforce memory restrictions. The kernel may terminate a container if it requires more memory than it can handle. But only when the kernel senses memory strain do terminations take place. As a result, a container that overallocates memory might not be terminated right away. Thus, memory limitations are applied in a reactive manner. If a container uses more memory than it is allowed to, it may be terminated.

2.3.2 Resource scheduling steps

The following crucial actions can be summarized as a sequence for scheduling resources.

- Breaking down the project scope into the list of tasks that need to be finished and calculating how long each task will take (in man-hours, days, or hours).
- Determining the limitations of each assignment, such as a due date, specific competencies needed to finish the task, staff availability, etc.
- Calculating the resource demand, or the kinds and quantities of resources needed to finish each task.
- Examining the capability of resources, including how much work they normally complete each day, their projected and actual workload, any scheduled vacation days, new recruits, etc.
- Assigning each resource to carry out a certain task on a given date by matching available resources with the tasks mentioned. The work will be delayed and rescheduled for the times when the employee is available if there are no other options and the resource is unable to do it.

2.3.3 Importance of Resource Scheduling

Scheduling resources in project management allows you to minimize resource overload by scheduling projects with resource constraints in mind.

The following benefits of resource scheduling are discernible.

- Because the team members are aware of the due dates for their tasks, the workflow is more predictable for them.
- Effective resource scheduling ensures a more balanced workload, reduces the likelihood of overload, and promotes more effective resource utilization by taking team members' capacities into consideration.

- A project manager will find it simpler to keep an eye on the whole project timeline to ensure that no deadlines are missed.
- If material resources are needed to finish the project, scheduling them will be a good strategy to guarantee their availability and appropriate allocation across project tasks, which lowers the likelihood of delays.

2.3.4 Resource Management

In order to guarantee that applications operate well, Kubernetes resource management entails supervising the distribution and use of hardware resources within a Kubernetes cluster. Because Kubernetes depends on a container orchestration system that can potentially manage thousands of containers on numerous servers, this management is necessary.

Managing Kubernetes resources requires the possibility to monitor and regulate the use of CPU, memory, storage, and network resources. The concepts and methods that allow Kubernetes to make this possible include pods, nodes and the control plane, among a few others.

The significance of Kubernetes resource management.

Kubernetes resource management ensures that the hardware resources are used efficiently and thus reduces the cost of operation. Although it is important to maintain the required level of performance and availability, proper management allows allocating the resources based on the specific needs of applications.

Kubernetes can optimize resource availability and recycling with the help of management resources. This enhances the performance of the system, besides avoiding the depletion of resources and aiding the scalability needs of containerized programmed in different settings.

2.3.5 Kubernetes compute resources

These are a few of the primary Kubernetes compute resources to keep an eye on.

- **CPU**

CPU units are used in Kubernetes to quantify CPU resources. Depending on the underlying architecture and cloud provider, one CPU in Kubernetes terminology might refer to either a single core or a hyperthread on a multicore computer. apps have adequate power to run without squandering resources that could be used by other apps when CPU resources are managed precisely.

Administrators can set CPU utilization restrictions and requests using management tools. As a result, an application or container can define the least amount of resources it needs (requests) and the most it can use (limits). This helps avoid CPU resource monopolization by a single application, which is important in multi-tenant setups.

- **Memory**

The management of memory in Kubernetes involves the allocation and limitation of the available RAM to pods and containers. Right-sizing prevents the cases of excessive use of memory that may affect other applications in a node. To avoid crashes in the system due to out-of-memory (OOM) issues, one should establish the right requests and restrictions.

The requests provided by Kubernetes give a guarantee of minimum required amounts of memory to ensure that the apps will have the necessary memory to run correctly and consistently. A memory restriction ensures that there is no overuse of memory by the programs when it is not required.

- **Ephemeral storage**

Storage directly associated with the life of the pod is known as ephemeral storage in Kubernetes. It is primarily applied to short-term data, e.g., caching layers and scratch data that are tightly integrated with some applications on the platform. To prevent the loss of data in the event of a pod failure or termination, it is necessary to control ephemeral storage.

Just like the CPU and RAM, Kubernetes allows the administrator to establish requests and restrictions of ephemeral storage. This will ensure that the space used in temporary storage is not surpassed by its allocation, which may impact on other processes.

2.4 Fault-Tolerant and High Availability Design

The concepts of high availability and fault tolerance are imperative aspects of IT infrastructure solutions that would ensure that businesses experience unbroken operations and minimal downtimes. The world of technology is dynamic and requires a strong IT infrastructure to enable the business to operate and be in a position to respond to the changing needs of the clients. Fault tolerance and high availability are two terms that are important in understanding when selecting the best infrastructure solution to use in your company.

Fault tolerance is the ability of an IT infrastructure to continue functioning despite failures on a part or unexpected interruptions. This may include network crashes, software failure or hardware failure. Fault tolerance is achieved through such techniques as redundancy, used in a system like mirroring data storage or installing backup power, among others.

High availability, in its turn, minimizes service disruption as it ensures the system is always available and operational. It eliminates issues such as planned upgrades and maintenance by implementing failover systems that automatically redirect workloads to other resources in case primary ones are unavailable. High availability often relies on load balancing and clustering techniques in order to divide work between multiple servers successfully.

Comparing fault tolerance and high availability, one will see that these two are not aimed at achieving the same purpose, but they both significantly enhance the overall system reliability. High-availability infrastructures ensure a higher priority on maintaining services running even when they are being subject to planned maintenance or even potential bottlenecks, whereas fault-tolerant systems put more emphasis on continuing to run even when they are subject to unexpected breakdowns. The IT infrastructure solution to adopt depends on the needs and specifications of a company.

As an example, due to the rigid legality of data protection and service availability, companies operating in intensively-regulated industries such as finance or healthcare can afford fault tolerance more than high availability. Conversely, those companies offering web-based services might be more inclined towards the high-availability solutions as they need to ensure high-level performance and fast response of end users.

In the case of a business that tries to maximize system resiliency and minimize hardware/software outages and accidental downtimes, focusing on fault tolerance and high availability may also prove to be an effective approach. Companies can ensure that their ITs can handle various challenges and maintain their levels of service quality by employing a hybrid infrastructure design integrating fault tolerance and high availability.

2.4.1 Understanding Fault Tolerance

Every person dealing with a computer system must learn the concept of fault tolerance, particularly those who should be in control of ensuring the soundness and integrity of data transmission and storage.

Essentially, fault tolerance is the ability of a system to continue operating well even when any or all of the components fail or suffer an error in the system. This notion is vital in the contemporary world, where data security and system reliability are highly important.

One way to get the meaning of fault tolerance is to compare it with redundancy. Redundancy is the process of copying vital parts or functions contained within a system in a way that will enable another part to replace the other part in the event of failure. Redundancy has become a typical element of a fault-tolerant design strategy. One of the ways to contribute to fault tolerance is through it, but it is not faulting tolerance. The fault-tolerant systems are utilized in numerous industries that require the data security and the high rates of reliability. An example of this is the common use of these systems in the servers of financial institutions and aviation control systems where accuracy and availability is most important to the business.

There are a number of strategies that developers can use when developing fault-tolerant systems, each having distinct benefits depending on specific applications and requirements, which include:

In the same way, n-version programming, a software module can be created in dozens of independently coded versions. Subsequently these different versions are concurrently run on other hardware of the system. The alternative versions may continue running in case one of the versions fails or meets with an error, as the entire system keeps on running.

To do it, the modular architecture that allows replacing faulty components with ease without disrupting the overall efficiency of the system or adding self-healing mechanisms to system components that involve monitoring signs of their degradation and replacing them in a timely manner.

The key point is to consider such factors as cost, complexity, and performance trade-offs of constructing fault-tolerant systems irrespective of the implementation techniques.

2.4.2 Understanding High Availability

High availability is another concept that is significant in technology and computers. It is the strategizing and implementation of processes and systems that ensure smooth functioning with minimal failure periods.

The high-availability solutions aim to provide uninterrupted access to data, applications, and services by avoidance of potential failure of the systems prior to their occurrence. This is achieved through redundancy, fault tolerance, load balancing and other mechanisms that work together to ensure that optimum performance is achieved.

Cloud computing allows businesses to provide and consume high-availability systems by providing scalable, reliable and cost-effective solutions that can be changed through dynamic needs and demands. Due to the high availability of cloud computing, applications, data storage and other services are available even when hardware breaks down or the system fails. This is enabled by multiple redundancies, which is the duplication of important elements within a system so that another can easily play the role in case of a system failure.

A number of factors lead to creation of high availability cloud environment, which include:

Virtual servers. These are often virtualized in multiple physical servers to give them high availability. Failure or breakdown of one physical server or going offline to be serviced can easily be diverted to another server without affecting the experience of the end user. This is enabled through virtualization technology which enables multiple virtual servers to use one physical server, this gives the result as an architecture that is more effective and scalable.

- **Monitoring.** Potential issues, e.g., bottlenecks, resource constraints, etc., can be identified at an early stage and preventive measures can be taken to avoid the escalation and ensuing downtime

- **Load balancing.** To ensure that there is no overloading or overwhelming of any resource, this involves sharing the work load of a number of resources (such as servers). It is also beneficial in maintaining stability of the system and making the most out of the available resources. To ensure high availability, load balancers are typically employed to distribute the network traffic entering the servers to various servers based on various algorithms and settings. This will make sure that all the servers are equally burdened.
- **Failover mechanisms**. These processes ensure that there will be a backup system part that will automatically step in the case of failure or issue without involving end users. Some of the infrastructure layers where failover may be experienced include the hardware, network and application layers just to name a few.

2.5 Cluster Design Principles and Design Best Practices

Cluster design principles are geared towards designing resilient and scalable, manageable systems to manage complex and typically cloud-native workloads. Among the main principles is high availability via redundancy and fault tolerance where resources such as control plane nodes, and data replicas are spread out across several availability zones or physical hosts to avoid single point failures. Scalability is considered another important value, where the system needs to be able to add or remove resources such as adding a worker node or changing replicas in a pod as demand varies without human intervention.

The principles are brought into implementation strategies as best practice in cluster design. These include the operational automation of deploying and operating which is one of these big practices, and involves applying infrastructure-as-code (IaC) platforms to provide consistency, reproducibility, and less human error across environments.

It is necessary to implement a full monitoring and observability stack, collecting metrics, logs, and traces to offer in-depth details about the state of the clusters, performance hotspots, and security incidents.

2.5.1 Design Principles of Computer Clusters

Clusters ought to be built with availability and scalability in mind.

1. Single-System Image Features

Unlike an SMP or a workstation, an operating system image stored in memory in a single copy is not referred to as SSI. Rather, it describes how symmetry, transparency, and a single control occur in a single system, as explained in the list below:

- **Single system**: Users perceive the whole bunch as a single machine with several processors. "Use five processors to execute my application," the user could say. This system is not the same as a distributed system.
- **Single control**: It makes sense for a system user or end user to access services from a single location using a single interface. For example, from a single control point, while a user submits batch jobs to a single set of queues, a system administrator configures all of the cluster's hardware and software.
- **Symmetry**: Any node can be used by a user to access a cluster service. To put it another way, every cluster service and feature is equal for every node and every user, with the exception of those who have access rights.
- **Location-transparent:** The location of the actual device that ultimately renders a service is unknown to the user. A tape drive connected to any cluster node, for example, can be used by the user as if it were physically connected to the local node.

The primary reason for having SSI is that it makes it possible to use, manage, and maintain a cluster in the same way as a familiar workstation. In "single-system image," "single" can occasionally be used interchangeably with either "global" or "central." For instance, a user can access a single file hierarchy from any node in a global file system. The cluster system can be configured and monitored by an operator from a single point of control. Even if a cluster service or capacity appears to be a single system, it is frequently carried out by the collaboration of several components in a dispersed manner. The primary requirement (and benefit) of SSI approaches is that they offer the usability advantages of a single picture along with the performance advantages of dispersed implementation.

2. Single Entry Point

With its single-entry point, single file hierarchy, single I/O space, single networking scheme, single control point, single memory space, single process space, single task management system, and single file hierarchy, the single-system image (SSI) is a very rich idea. Even though the cluster may have multiple physical host nodes to service the login sessions, the single-entry point allows users to log in as a single virtual host (for example, via Telnet, rlogin, or HTTP). To share the load, the system transparently divides user login and connection requests among several physical hosts. Mainframes and supercomputers could be replaced by clusters. Additionally, thousands of HTTP or FTP requests may arrive at once on an Internet cluster server. It's not easy to set up a single-entry point with several hosts. Numerous problems need to be fixed. Just a portion of the list is as follows:

- **Home directory:** Where should the user's home directory be located?
- **Verification:** How are user logins authenticated?
- **Several connections:** What happens if the same user logs into the same account many times?
- **Failure of the host:** When one or more hosts fail, how do you handle it?

After translating the symbolic name, the DNS provides the least-loaded node's IP address, 159.226.41.150, which is node Host1. After that, the user uses this IP address to log in. To make decisions about load-balancing translation, the host nodes provide load data to the DNS on a regular basis. Ideally, if there are 200 users, the login sessions are split equally among our hosts log in at once, each of whom has 50 users. This makes it possible for one host to have four times the power.

3. Single File Hierarchy

In this book, the phrase "single file hierarchy" refers to the appearance of a single, massive file system image that seamlessly blends local and global discs with different file devices, such tapes. To put it another way, the root directory / contains a few subdirectories that house all of the files a user needs, and common UNIX commands like open, read, and so on can be used to access them. A workstation's many file systems existing as subdirectories of the root directory should not be confused with this.

The disc on a process's local node is known as local storage. Remote storage is provided by the discs on distant nodes. Two things are necessary for a stable storage system: It is fault-tolerant to some extent by employing redundancy and recurring backup to tapes, and it is persistent, meaning that data will remain in the stable storage for a long enough amount of time (for example, a week) even after the cluster goes down. Stable storage files are referred to as global files, local storage files as local files, and remote storage files as remote files. One huge, centralized RAID disc might be used for stable storage. However, cluster nodes' local discs could also be used for distribution. The first method makes use of a big disc, which could be a single point of failure and a performance snag. Although the latter strategy is more challenging to execute, it may be more accessible, cost-effective, and efficient.

2.5.2 High Availability Cluster

Groups of hosts, or actual computers, that operate as a single system and offer constant availability are known as high-availability clusters. Databases, e-commerce websites, and transaction processing systems are examples of mission-critical applications that require high-availability clusters.

High-availability clusters are commonly utilized for failover, backup, and load balancing. Every host in a high-availability (HA) cluster needs to have access to the same shared storage in order for it to operate correctly. If a virtual machine (VM) on one host has downtime, it can seamlessly switch to another host.

Storage administrators should be mindful that adding too many virtual machines and hosts to a single cluster may make load balancing challenging, even if a high-availability cluster may include anything from two to dozens of nodes.

Clusters of servers that support services or applications that must operate reliably with little downtime are known as high-availability server clusters.

High-availability designs use redundant software that is placed on several machines and performs a similar function so that each machine can serve as a backup in the event that another component fails. If a website or application breaks without this clustering, the service won't be accessible until it is fixed.

This circumstance is avoided by an existing architecture with the following procedure:

- Detecting failure
- Carrying out application failover to an additional redundant host
- Restarting or fixing the malfunctioning server without the need for human assistance

2.5.3 Clustering: Best practices

Queue managers can be connected through the use of clusters.

1. **General Design Considerations**

- **Strive for Simplicity:** Distributed systems are inherently complex. Make minimalism your top priority while designing for a number of reasons. Reduce the number of "moving parts" and avoid distributing algorithms among several objects.
- **Minimize Remote Calls:** Reducing remote calls enhances performance and lessens the impact of failures.

2. **Session Facades Reduce Remote Calls**

Stay away from using client or servlet code to access EJB entity beans. Instead, limit calls from Web apps to RMI objects by using A session bean, also known as a façade, aids in containing intricate interactions. Every getter method is a remote call when an entity bean is accessed directly by a client application. The entity bean can be accessed locally by a session facade bean, which can then gather the data in a structure and return it by value.

3. **Transfer Objects Reduce Remote Calls**

It's doubtful that EJBs will work best for every item in an application because they require a lot of system resources and network bandwidth to run.

Logical groupings of information and related business logic can be modelled using EJBs, for example, to simulate a rational subset of an invoice's line items. Use an EJB, such as those that are subject to taxes, rebates, discounts, or other changes.

A single line item on an invoice, on the other hand, is fine-grained; it wastes network resources to implement it as an EJB. To express a group of data fields that only require get and set operations, use transfer objects.

When modelling entities that have a collection of properties that are always accessible together, Transfer objects, sometimes referred to as aid classes or value objects, are useful. Within an EJB, A serializable class called a transfer object combines related properties to create a composite value. A remote business method's return type is this class.

Clients access the transfer object's fine-grained values locally after obtaining instances of this class through the use of coarse-grained business methods. Multiple values can be fetched in a single server round-trip, which reduces latency, network traffic, and server resource use.

4. Distributed Transactions Increase Remote Calls

Steer clear of transactions involving many instances of the server. Distributed transactions, in addition to utilizing network overhead and capacity for resource coordination, make remote calls.

5. Web Application Design Considerations

- **Configure In-Memory Replication:** Session state must remain in memory for servlets and JSPs to have automatic failover. To set up in-memory replication for HTTP session states, follow these steps:
- **Design for Idempotence:** Session state must remain in memory for servlets and JSPs to have automatic failover. To set up in-memory replication for HTTP session states, follow these steps:

Multiple-Choice Questions (MCQs)

1. **What is the primary advantage of a multi-cluster Kubernetes architecture?**

   A) Reduces container image size
   B) Improves fault isolation and disaster recovery
   C) Eliminates the need for worker nodes
   D) Prevents all application failures

2. **In Kubernetes, what is the main purpose of horizontal scaling?**

   A) Increasing CPU and memory of an existing node or pod
   B) Adding more replicas or nodes to handle increased load
   C) Compressing workloads to save storage
   D) Reducing network latency by disabling services

3. **Which of the following best describes vertical scaling?**

   A) Adding more pods to a deployment
   B) Increasing the resource capacity of an existing pod or node
   C) Creating more namespaces
   D) Replicating the control plane across clusters

4. **What is the key role of the Kubernetes scheduler?**

   A) Managing container images
   B) Assigning pods to appropriate nodes based on constraints and resources
   C) Creating YAML manifests automatically
   D) Encrypting cluster communication

5. **Which Kubernetes feature helps ensure workloads are distributed across nodes for better resilience?**

   A) ConfigMaps
   B) Secrets
   C) Pod Anti-Affinity
   D) Ingress Controller

6. **What is a major characteristic of a fault-tolerant system?**

   A) It shuts down immediately when one component fails
   B) It continues operating even when some components fail
   C) It uses only one master node
   D) It avoids using replicas to save resources

7. **Which design approach improves high availability in Kubernetes clusters?**

   A) Running all workloads on a single node
   B) Using multiple control plane nodes
   C) Disabling health checks
   D) Avoiding persistent storage

8. **Which of the following is a best practice for resource management in Kubernetes?**

   A) Avoid setting resource requests and limits
   B) Schedule all workloads on the same node
   C) Define resource requests and limits for containers
   D) Use only default scheduling for every workload

9. **Why are liveness and readiness probes important in resilient application design?**

   A) They increase container image size
   B) They help Kubernetes detect unhealthy containers and manage traffic properly
   C) They replace the need for autoscaling
   D) They prevent the use of persistent volumes

10. **Which principle is most important in cluster design for large-scale Kubernetes environments?**

   A) Centralizing all workloads on one machine
   B) Designing for scalability, redundancy, and failure recovery
   C) Disabling node communication for security
   D) Using only vertical scaling

Answer

1	2	3	4	5	6	7	8	9	10
B	B	B	B	C	B	B	C	B	B

Chapter 3

Kubernetes Networking And Storage At Scale

3.1 Ingress, Egress and Traffic Control

In general computer science, ingress and egress refer to the incoming and outgoing traffic in a computer system or network. Platform teams may manage traffic into and out of the Kubernetes cluster using a controlled manner thanks to Kubernetes ingress and egress. This element is essential to the operation of highly scalable and secure production settings. The flow of external users or systems into a Kubernetes cluster is known as ingress, which is usually based on either HTTP or HTTPS (both of which use the TCP protocol). Instead of defining ingress rules by listing individual services to the internet, organizations use an Ingress resource to define ingress rules. Typically, this resource is set up in YAML format, which guides traffic through Kubernetes should be directed according to specifications such as URL routes or domain names.

Data egress is the process by which data moves from a network to an external place. One kind of network activity that poses a risk to organizations is network data egress in the case where it reveals sensitive data to a wrong or unintended recipient. Egress occurs any time information comes out of the network of a particular organization, whether it is via email messages, uploaded data either through "File Transfer Protocol" (FTP) or "Hypertext Transfer Protocol" (HTTP) transfers, or through a file stored on portable media such as "Universal Serial Bus" (USB) devices and external hard drives.

3.1.1 Benefits of ingress in Kubernetes

1. **Cost efficiency:** Particularly in microservices systems with numerous independently deployed apps, Ingress lowers the cost of IT infrastructure by enabling different services to share a single external load balancer.
2. **Simplified operations:** Reducing administrative complexity and ensuring consistency across services are two benefits of centralized routing, domain configuration, and certificate administration.
3. **Enhanced security:** Policies such as rate restriction, authentication, or web application firewalls can be enforced consistently, and SSL/TLS termination for incoming traffic takes place at a single control point. By enforcing security checks before traffic reaches backend services, this configuration helps prevent typical security problems like unauthorised access.
4. **Better scalability:** Expanding services behind a single, adaptable entry point is simple with Ingress's support for path- and hostname-based routing. For instance, teams can scale services autonomously without adding new external destinations when routing is based on API pathways.

3.1.2 Benefits of egress in Kubernetes

1. **Strong data protection:** By limiting outbound traffic, egress network controls lessen the possibility of data leaks or compromised services connecting to nefarious external endpoints.
2. **Compliance:** By restricting connections to authorized endpoints and offering insight into audits, managing Kubernetes' egress traffic guarantees that sensitive workloads satisfy legal requirements.
3. **Better cost control**: Egress traffic management helps avoid unforeseen cloud fees from massive data transfers or uncontrolled outbound calls.
4. **Improved observability**: Vendor management, debugging, and detecting external service dependencies are all made possible by managing egress traffic, which provides visibility into which external systems apps rely on.

3.1.3 Best Practices for Data Egress Management

Finding out where Data egress control depends on where private information is kept and how it exits the network. This procedure is known as network monitoring and data discovery, is essential to protecting an organization's system's data egress points.

To do this, the following are best practices:

1. **Design a data egress enforcement policy:** Organisations must develop and adhere to data egress enforcement rules that define acceptable data use. This policy needs to be quite detailed and explain how the company gets its resources and listing the services that are available online which the company has agreed to be used and the methods that the employees use to get sensitive information and how they manage it.

2. **Monitor networks:** Making sure to keep an eye on the activity on an organization's network is the first step in guaranteeing secure data egress. This enables an organization to detect any unusual activity in addition to knowing which users and devices are connected to its network. Additionally, network monitoring is a method through which organizations can measure such important metrics as availability, response time, and uptime.
3. **Install a powerful firewall:** Network controllers, or firewalls, assist a company in managing data entry and exit effectively. Most data breaches were left to take place due to the toxin rules of many organizations that enabled intruders access and intercept data without the company having the slightest idea that an attacker was active in their systems.
4. **Apply firewall policy:** Having an efficient network firewall in place is one thing but must be accompanied by proper rules to allow it to identify, evaluate and intercept any unwanted information leakage. Good firewall policies will enable an organization to prevent the departure of data to unauthorized destinations and malicious persons.
5. **Implement firewall logging:** To control and protect against harmful activity, egress and ingress data flow should be recorded. Using "security information and event management" (SIEM) systems, firewall logging enables a company to examine its network traffic. These instruments allow them to assemble, match and control information across their networks and systems and when properly configured, the same solutions will aid them in avoiding the exposure of their data illegally.
6. **Secure sensitive information:** It is important that organizations determine their sensitive information and provide classification labels on the same that determine the degree of protection that the information needs. This is what is referred to as data discovery and classification, where a company can locate, classify, and take appropriate security precautions for its most sensitive data. Before deciding on the level of security they require and to whom they should grant access to particular information and

resources , businesses must identify, locate, and arrange their sensitive information.

7. **Implement data loss prevention:** Businesses can make use of "data loss prevention" (DLP) solutions to safeguard their sensitive data after learning about data classification. DLP employs policy-based protection, such as data encryption or barring unauthorised activity, to safeguard sensitive data. When DLP is used in tandem Businesses will have a thorough grasp of their sensitive data, including where it is stored and how it is safeguarded against loss, thanks to data classification and discovery and unauthorised disclosure.
8. **Restrict data access:** It is not only enough to protect data, but also to control all parties' access to resources, networks, and data. To accomplish this, a business should be put in place and adhere to an authorization policy which will make sure that any device that will be linked to a network must first be granted before joining the network.
9. **Incident response:** The organizations must have a predetermined incident response in case of a breach of data or a data leakage. The best method of ensuring the safety of the company against an attack is by having a thorough incident response plan that provides future actions that can be repeated and defines who is supposed to be doing the needed action. It allows organizations to reduce the harm that a cyberattack will have and reduce the threat as swiftly as possible. The proper incident response strategy in addition to involves the investigation of what occurred which plays a significant role in learning the attack and planning on future occurrence.

3.1.4 Kubernetes Ingress and Egress Networking and Traffic Controlling

The incoming (ingress) and the outgoing (egress) traffic should operate efficiently in the Kubernetes clusters to communicate with the external environment. Kubernetes Ingress is controlled by Ingress Controllers that locate external requests that are made using HTTP/HTTPS and map them to internal services. These controllers are mandatory in routing user traffic not within the cluster such as load balancing and service exposure. The recommendation now is to apply to the Kubernetes Gateway API and Gateway resources, where the traditional Ingress resources are preferred due to the ability to control and to scale. The selection of the appropriate Ingress Controller, either NGINX, Traefik, or Envoy Gateway, may have a profound influence on traffic flow and scalability.

Egress controls communication out of pods with external resources, such as APIs or databases. Security and performance are achieved by configuring Network Policies, Egress Gateways, to access external networks. Egress is also reliant on controllers installed in Kubernetes and controlling outbound traffic. These elements guarantee that communication within the cluster is restricted to authorized services only, which is another control overlay to the architecture.

In case we must put in place an Ingress and Egress gateway control then it is advisable to utilize Istio. The solution of Istio is a complete one that can be used to control both incoming and outgoing traffic, which has improved security, observability, and traffic control features.

Ingress and Egress, along with each other, make up a fully-fledged architecture that ensures and streamlines how Kubernetes clusters communicate with the internal and external environment. Ingress and egress strategies can be planned well to enhance the reliability of our applications, security, and efficiency of Kubernetes.

3.2 Load Balancing and Service Discovery

When it comes to negotiating the intricacies of a microservices architecture, static service discovery techniques like hardcoding service locations or employing load balancers fall short.

Microservices can find and connect to the right instances of other services they need to communicate with thanks to service discovery techniques.

These systems become extremely sophisticated and challenging to administer when they are required to locate and connect instances across microservices.

Microservices architecture is best served by dynamic service discovery, such as service registries and service meshes. Because services may find each other without locations being hardcoded, they provide loose coupling, which keeps the distribution system flexible. By rerouting traffic over failed instances, they also incorporated resilience.

3.2.1 Service Discovery

The technology used to automatically identify the process of locating devices and services is known as service discovery on a computer network. It is the process by which microservices and apps find various network components. This technique is implemented using a network protocol called a service discovery protocol, which lessens the amount of manual configuration work that administrators and users must do.

to put in place client-server and central server service discovery. All that is needed is a common language that enables the applications to utilise each other's services without the need for further user participation.

We must manage service instances with changing locations when developing a microservices application. Depending on autoscaling, service updates, and failures, these instances may also need to be modified during runtime. The services that rely on these instances need to be informed of this situation.

Let's say you are writing code that uses a REST API to call a service. To submit a request, the code requires the service instance's IP address and port. These locations don't need to be looked for at any point if your application is hardware-based.

The number of instances in a microservice design, however, will differ, and their locations won't be recorded in a configuration file. Because of this, it is challenging to determine how many services are available at any given time. To find service instances in dynamically allocated network locations in a cloud-based microservices location, people require service discovery in microservices.

All instances benefit from being able to adjust and distribute the load appropriately. There are three parts to service discovery.

- A business that provides services through a network is called a service provider.
- A database that lists every service's location is called a service registry instance.
- A service consumer that interacts with the service instance and locates the service provider using the service registry.

3.2.2 Types of Service Discovery

Client-side and server-side discovery are the two main paradigms of service discovery. Each of them has applications, benefits, and drawbacks of its own. The main distinction is that the client bears the responsibility for locating available service instances in client-side discovery, whereas the server bears this obligation in server-side discovery.

1. Client-Side Service Discovery

To find a service provider the customer or service client in this type of service discovery must look through the service registration. Next, using a load balancing technique, the client chooses an appropriate and free service instance to submit a request. In this approach, Once the service has started, the service registry has a record of the service instance's location. When the service instance is ended, the location data is removed. A heartbeat mechanism is used to perform this refresh on a regular basis.

Because the customer is still aware of which service instances are accessible and able to handle the load, this kind enables us to make wise decisions about load balancing. It is simple to understand and allows the client to determine the network locations of available service instances.

A central server that acts as a phone book for every service instance that is available is called a discovery server, receives the client's initial query. Additionally, it gives the service instances an additional layer of abstraction.

The service may be positioned behind an API gateway in client-side service discovery. If not, the client is in charge of putting features like cross-cutting, balancing, and authentication into practice.

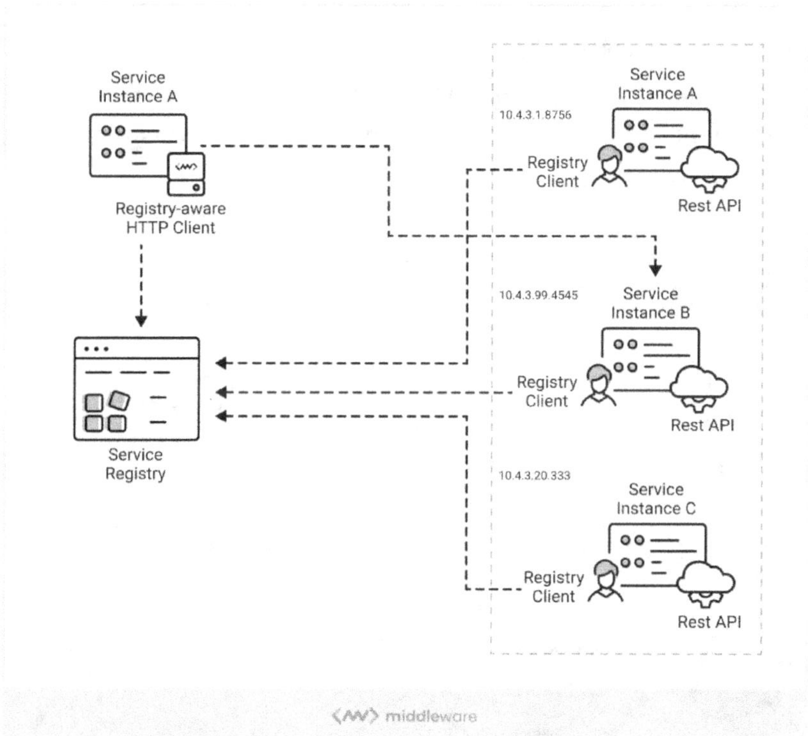

Figure 3.1: Client-Side Service Discovery
Source: (Shah, 2025)

2. **Server-Side Service Discovery**

The customer or the client is not required to know about the service registry in order to use this kind of service discovery. After receiving the requests, a router looks for the service registry itself. The router passes the request and completes the task when it locates a legitimate service that is available.

The client doesn't must be concerned about finding a suitable service or load balancing, for example, in this paradigm. Rather, the API gateway does this task by choosing the appropriate endpoint for a request originating from the client.

In essence, the server side is in charge of receiving and successfully forwarding the client server's request. This is accomplished by keeping track various service locations and determining the client's preferred service without requiring manual participation from the customer.

Every client request is handled similarly by the load balancer. The service instances are registered with the service registry at service startup, much as client-side discovery. As soon as the service is terminated, the instance is deregistered.

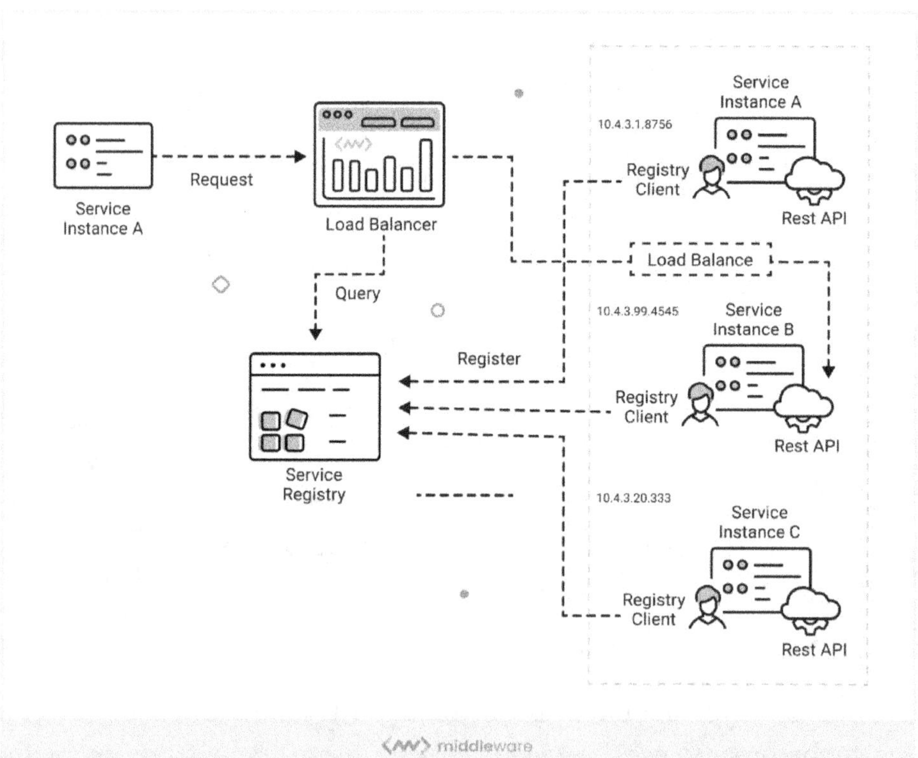

Figure 3.2: Server-Side Service Discovery
Source: (Shah, 2025)

3.2.3 What is a service registry?

The instances and network locations of any service that is provided are kept up to date in a centralised database called a service registry, which then makes them accessible for application-level communication. After indicating their availability by registering with the database, services search the registry for any instances they require.

What is the operation of a service registry?

1. Services become discoverable by registering themselves when they go online.
2. A service queries the registry to connect to the correct instance when it wants to find and establish a connection with one.
3. To guarantee that a client receives information that links it to healthy instances, the registry is updated to reflect the shifting environment as services come and go.

3.2.4 Key features of a service registry

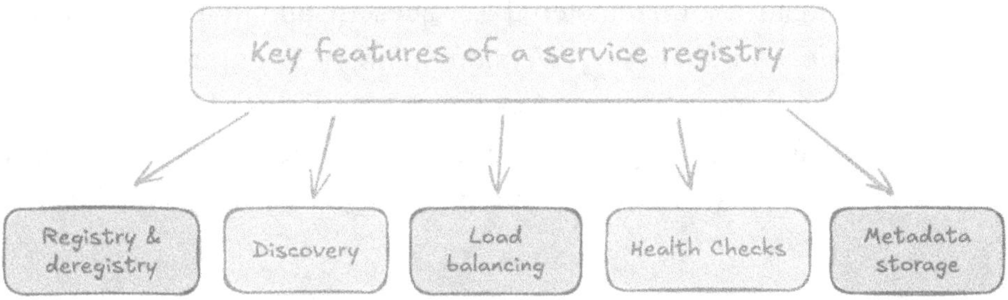

Figure 3.3: Features of a Service Registry
Source: (Baran, 2024)

- **Registry and deregister**: A service instance registers its network location (IP address and port) with the start-up service registry. To avoid additional services from trying to connect to it, a service instance deregisters itself from the service registry when it shuts down or becomes unhealthy (i.e., non-responsive).
- **Discovery:** Without hardcoding network locations, service registries enable dynamic discovery of service endpoints. Services search the registry for instances of other services rather than having a fixed network location where instances can be located.
- **Load balancing:** The majority of service registries use load balancers. They divide traffic among several service instances in order to distribute it evenly. This improves fault tolerance and performance.
- **Health checks:** A health check URL is usually one of the built-in health check mechanisms found in many service registries. The registry then queries the URL on a regular basis to confirm the health of registered service instances. It gets deregistered if an unhealthy instance is discovered.
- **Metadata storage** Registries have the ability to maintain metadata about registered services in addition to registering services for discovery. Version numbers, configuration settings, and custom attributes are examples of this data that can be used to route requests according to particular criteria or offer comprehensive information for debugging and monitoring.

3.2.5 Load Balancing

The technique of distributing computing duties among two or more machines is known as load balancing. Load balancing is a commonly used technique on the Internet to distribute network traffic among multiple servers. Each server becomes less stressed and more effective as a result, which enhances performance and reduces latency. For the majority of Internet applications to operate correctly, load balancing is necessary.

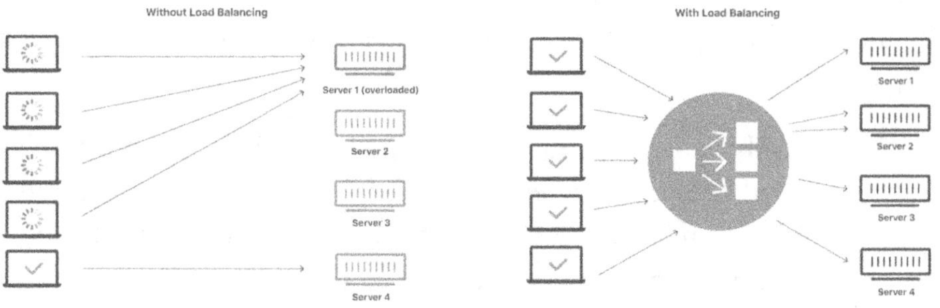

Figure 3.4: Load Balancing Architecture
Source: (Cloudflare, 2025)

Consider a grocery store checkout queue where there are eight lines, and there's only one open. Because everyone must wait in the same queue, Customers take a long time to complete their grocery payment. Imagine that all eight checkout lines are suddenly open at the store. In this case, wait times for customers are about eight times shorter (depending on factors like how much food each client is buying).

Essentially, the same goal is achieved by load balancing. User wait times are significantly reduced by distributing user enquiries among several servers. This enhances the user experience; if the customers of the grocery store in the previously described example consistently had to wait a long period, they would likely seek out a more efficient food store.

The technology or program that manages load balancing is called a load balancer. Load balancers come in two varieties: software-based and hardware-based. Software-based load balancers can run on a server, virtual machine, or cloud, while hardware load balancers need a specialized load balancing device to be installed. Load balancing is a common use for "content delivery networks" (CDN).

After receiving a user request, the load balancer sends it to a particular server; this procedure is repeated for each request. Load balancers use a variety of techniques to choose which server should handle each request techniques. The two main categories of these algorithms are dynamic and static.

As was already noted, Web applications frequently employ load balancing. Load balancers, whether software-based or cloud-based, aid in distributing Internet traffic among the servers hosting the application in an equitable manner. “Global server load balancing” (GSLB) is a technology that allows some cloud load balancing systems to distribute Internet traffic loads among servers situated all over the world.

Large, localized networks, such those in data centers or expansive office buildings, frequently use load balancing. Hardware appliances like an application delivery controller (ADC) or a specialist load balancing device are typically needed for this. For this purpose, software-based load balancers are also employed.

3.3 Enduring Storage and CSI Structures

The simplest form of storage in Kubernetes is fleeting, or non-persistent. Every Ephemeral storage, a transient directory on the host of the Kubernetes pod, is by default present in the container computer. It isn’t transportable or long-lasting.

Persistent storage is also another type of storage supported by Kubernetes. This may involve cloud providers (e.g., Amazon S3), stowage strategies in the resident datacenter or statistics service (e.g., databases). Kubernetes offers a way of abstracting this storage to applications that run on containers, to ensure that applications do not ever talk to storage media.

CSI is a Kubernetes extension that offers simplicity to the storage management. Prior to CSI, users had to do the integration of the device driver of the data store and Kubernetes which was a bit tricky. CSI offers a pluggable architecture, thus being able to include plugins that are compatible with the organization’s storage devices and services easily.

CSI is a Kubernetes extension, which makes storage management easier. Before CSI, customers had to combine the device driver of the data store with Kubernetes, which was incredibly challenging. CSI gives it extensible architecture of plugins, hence making it easy to add a certain type of plugin to support the organization's storage devices and services. Non-persistent (temporary) storage is what Kubernetes uses by default. Therefore, if a container is available, it stores the data in the host's temporary storage area, and when it is shut down, the data is deleted.

The name of this term is enduring storage as it focuses on the principle of data persistence that makes the data resistant to crashes of systems, power outages, and other disasters. The most important feature is that the information is not lost and can be accessed even when the computer is off or when the application that created the information is terminated as opposed to the temporary or volatile storage such as RAM.

3.3.1 Persistent Volumes (PV) and Persistent Volume Claims (PVC)

Two fundamental ideas are used by Kubernetes to allow persistent storage:

- **Persistent Volume (PV):** is a cluster storage component that can be manually defined by an administrator or dynamically defined by a storage class. A PV's lifecycle is different from a Kubernetes pod's. Details on how to implement storage for iSCSI, cloud provider-specific storage systems, or NFS is captured by the PV API.
- **Persistent Volume Claim (PVC):** is a user's storage request. A specific kind of storage can be requested by an application operating on a container. A container can, for instance, define the amount of storage space it requires or the method of data access (read-only, write-only, read/write, with one-time or continuous access).

Administrators have the option to provide PVs with unique characteristics, such as disc type HDD vs. SSD), storage tier (cold or normal), performance level, and storage space and access mode. Users can request storage based on these custom criteria without knowing the intricacies of how the underlying storage is implemented. The Storage Class resource is used to accomplish this.

- **Storage Classes**

To set up Storage Class and give each one a PV. One kind of storage is represented by a Storage Class. For instance, rapid SSD storage might be represented by one Storage Class, whereas magnetic drives or remote cloud storage might be represented by another. This enables Kubernetes clusters to set up many storage types in accordance with workload demands.

A Storage Class is a Kubernetes API that allows administrators to construct new volumes as needed by using dynamic configuration to configure storage parameters. In order for containers to communicate with the storage device, the volume plug-in, external provider (if any), and "container storage interface" (CSI) driver name are all specified by the Storage Class.

3.3.2 Kubernetes Storage Best Practices

1. Kubernetes Volumes Settings

No specific container in the cluster affects the "Persistent Volume" (PV) life cycle. A container user or application's request for a particular kind of storage is known as a "Persistent Volume Claim" (PVC).

Kubernetes advises the following while building a PV:

- PVCs should always be included in container configurations.
- A container will be strongly coupled to a particular volume if PVs are included in the container setup.

- PVCs will fail if they don't identify a certain class if there isn't a default Storage Class.
- Give Storage Classes names that have meaning.

2. Limiting Storage Resource Consumption

Limiting the quantity of storage that containers can use is recommended in order to reflect either the budget for cloud storage resources or the real amount of storage that is available in the local data center.

Container storage can be restricted in two primary ways:

- **Resource Quotas—** All containers within a Kubernetes namespace are restricted in their usage of resources, such as storage, CPU, and memory, by resource quotas.
- **Storage Classes**: in response to a PVC, a Storage Class has the ability to restrict the quantity of storage allocated to containers.

3. Resource Requests and Limits

To help control the amount of resources that each container is permitted to use, Kubernetes offers resource requests and resource limitations.

For temporary storage, a resource restriction can be set. Containers can avoid being limited by resource scarcity on container hosts or unexpectedly consuming too many resources by setting resource requests and restrictions.

To make sure that each container in a pod has resource demands and limits, use this command:

kubectl describe pod -n {your_namespace} {your_pod}

3.3.3 CSI Structures in Kubernetes

Whereas, before CSI Kubernetes offered an efficient volume plugin architecture, it was hard to enable Vendors who wanted to have their storage system supported by The Kubernetes release procedure has to be followed, even if it was merely to resolve a bug in a volume plugin. New volume plugins were also in-tree, which means that the core Kubernetes binaries incorporated their code. Furthermore, third-party storage code was generally challenging (and sometimes impossible) to assess and maintain, and thus resulted in security and reliability problems in core Kubernetes binaries by Kubernetes maintainers.

In order to expose containerized workloads to “Container Orchestration Systems” (COs) like as a standard, Kubernetes, CSI was created to provide arbitrary file and block storage systems. The Kubernetes volume layer is now really flexible thanks to the implementation of the Container Storage Interface. Without ever needing to modify the underlying Kubernetes code, third-party storage providers can use CSI to create and implement new storage systems in Kubernetes. This increases the storage options available to Kubernetes users and improves the system’s dependability and security.

3.3.4 How to use a CSI volume

CSI volumes can be used similarly to If a CSI storage plugin has been installed in a Kubernetes cluster, you can use Persistent Volume Claims, Persistent Volumes, and Storage Classes are examples of Kubernetes storage API objects.

The following option might be necessary even if Kubernetes CSI is used to introduce CSI as a GA feature in Kubernetes v1.13:

- Binaries for Kubelet and API servers: o--Allow-privileged=true Only privileged pods may perform bidirectional mount propagation, which is necessary for the majority of CSI plugins. Only in settings such as GCE, GKE, and Kubeadm, where this option is set to true do by default. —are privileged pods allowed.

1. Dynamic Provisioning

For plugins for CSI Storage that enable dynamic provisioning, the automatic generation and deletion of volumes can be enabled by establishing a Storage Class referencing the CSI plugin.

For instance, a CSI volume plugin called Storage Class allows the dynamic construction of "fast-storage" volumes "csi-driver.example. com." (CODE 1)

When volume provisioning is activated, the csi-driver.example.com CSI plugin receives a Create Volume call with the parameter type: pd-ssd and the secret or secrets that are referenced. In response, a new volume is provided by the external volume plugin, which then automatically creates a Persistent Volume something to symbolize it. Next, the newly created Persistent Volume object is bound to the Persistent Volume Claim by Kubernetes, enabling its use.

2. Pre-Provisioned Volumes

To manually create a Persistent Volume object to represent an existing volume in Kubernetes so that it is always exposed. For instance, the following Persistent Volume displays a volume from the CSI storage plugin is known as "existing Volume Name.""csi-driver.example.com." (CODE 2)

3.4 Networking Models and CNI Plugins with Kubernetes

Kubernetes networking is based on the "Container Network Interface" (CNI) standard, in which every pod has its own IP, and there is no need to use NAT, implemented by an optional CNI plug-in (such as Calico, Flannel) to configure network interfaces, routes, and policies to pods, services, and external connections. These node-managed containers runtime, meet the core network model of Kubernetes, enabling the use of a wide range of needs include overlay, host-based, or flat networks and support more advanced features such as network policies and dual-stack IP.

That is because the Kubernetes networking model specifies four different types of communication (external-to-service, pod-to-service, container-to-container, and pod-to-pod) and that CNI extensions are necessary to configure the network when pods are created, making sure that IP addresses are unique and that pods can be accessed directly. Various plugins have different capabilities, with simple overlay networks (Flannel) to richer solutions, with network policy enforcement and eBPF support at the edges (Cilium, Calico), giving administrators flexibility to find the best option to the needs of scalability, security, and particular cloud conditions.

3.4.1 Kubernetes Networking Model

The purpose of Kubernetes was designed to manage dispersed systems across a collection of computers. Because distributed systems are inherently distributed, networking is a vital component of Kubernetes deployment. It is possible to run, monitor, and troubleshoot Kubernetes applications correctly by understanding the Kubernetes networking paradigm.

In the vast subject of networking, there are numerous cutting-edge technologies. This can be unnerving for folks who are unfamiliar with the environment because there are many new and old concepts to comprehend and integrate into a coherent whole, and most individuals have preconceived ideas about networking. Technologies such as IP forwarding, virtual interfaces, network namespaces, and network address translation may be included in a non-exhaustive list.

Kubernetes makes subjective decisions on the networking of Pods. The following specifications are specifically imposed on any networking implementation by Kubernetes:

- Network address translation (NAT) is not required for communication between any two pods.
- Without NAT, every node can connect to every pod.
- A pod's perceived IP is the same as what other people perceive it to be.

Four different networking difficulties remain to be resolved in light of these limitations:

1. Networking between containers
2. Networking between pods
3. Networking via pod-to-service
4. Networking via the Internet

3.4.2 Network Plugins in Kubernetes

Cluster networking is made possible by "Container Network Interface" (CNI) plugins in Kubernetes (version 1.3 through the most recent version 1.35, and probably beyond). You need to utilize a CNI plugin compatible with your cluster that satisfies your requirements. The larger Kubernetes ecosystem offers a variety of plugins, both open-source and closed-source.

The Kubernetes network model cannot be implemented without a CNI plugin.

A CNI plugin that works with the CNI specification's v0.4.0 or later versions is required. Making use of a plugin that complies with the CNI specification v1.0.0 is advised by the Kubernetes project (plugins can be compatible with several spec versions).

Network Plugin Requirements:

1. **Loopback CNI**

For each sandbox (pod sandboxes, vm sandboxes, etc.), Kubernetes in order to implement the in addition to the CNI plugin deployed on the nodes, the container runtimes in the Kubernetes network model need to have a loopback interface. Reusing the CNI loopback plugin is one way to implement the loopback interface. or by creating your own code to accomplish this (see to this CRI-O example).

2. **Support HostPort**

HostPort is supported by the networking plugin for CNI. The CNI plugin team's official portmap plugin or your own port Mapping plugin capabilities are both options.

Port Mappings must be enabled in your cni-conf-dir, if you wish to enable hostPort support. For instance: (CODE 3)

3. **Support traffic shaping**

Pod ingress and egress traffic customization is also supported by the CNI networking plugin. You have the option of using your own plugin with bandwidth control features or the official bandwidth plugin provided by the CNI plugin team.

You must put the bandwidth plugin in your CNI bin directory (by default, /opt/cni/bin) and add it to your CNI configuration file (by default, /etc/cni/net.d) in order to enable traffic shaping capability.

3.5 Performance Issues in Deployments of Scale

These scalability issues can often be experienced with large-scale deployments with a combination of many external APIs where concurrent requests increase, response characteristics become heterogeneous and rate-limiting constraints are enforced by the upstream services. With the increase in system scale, the fixed configurations of middleware fail at either adapting to changes in traffic patterns which cause high response latency, early throughput saturation, and decreased service reliability. The bottlenecks are often the result of inefficient usage of caches, constraints of throttling policy and slow identification of failures, all of which increase tail latency and worsen the perceived performance of users in high-load conditions.

There is also a further problem in multi-source API environments, whereby the individual services have varying availability, update rates, and failure characteristics. In the absence of adaptive control mechanisms, the middleware systems cannot effectively balance performance optimization and fault tolerance leading to the cascading failures or non-optimal use of resources. As a result, middleware architectures that have the ability to monitor real-time performance, modify parameters on demand, and proactively handle failures are needed to facilitate scalable deployments where the service quality, SLA requirements, and predictable system behavior are expected to remain consistently high, as needed by the growing demand.

3.5.1 Challenges in Autoscaling while deployment

For any company that deals with varying traffic volumes, autoscaling is essential. It makes it possible for the servers to automatically modify their processing capacity in response to the present load. The server's capacity can be temporarily increased or decreased based on demand thanks to autoscaling. This increases the system's elasticity and responsiveness and lessens the need to forecast traffic levels.

Autoscaling maintains performance on the big days and saves money on the quiet ones.

Autoscaling accomplishes this, but it's a little more intricate than that. Additionally, autoscaling isn't the "cure-all" it seems, as anyone who manages a website with a lot of traffic is aware.

Even though many of the businesses who use Queue-it to avoid website breakdowns have autoscaling configured, they still experience problems during periods of high traffic.

1. Autoscaling is complex

The primary obstacle to effective autoscaling is the requirement to scale all crucial tech stack components in order to handle high traffic.

While it might be simple to scale cloud servers, it can be challenging, costly, and occasionally impossible to get every separate tech stack component to work either automatically or manually.

For instance, Canadian Health Center NLCHI believed that scaling their servers on AWS would be beneficial when they had significant surges in traffic.

However, “this just brought the bottleneck from the frontend to the backend,” as Director of Solution Development and Support Andrew Roberts explained to us.

This is just too typical. New bottlenecks nearly always appear as scaling occurs.

There are numerous possible sources of these blockages. Among the most prevalent ones we’ve observed are:

- Gateways for payments
- Database queries and locks (such as logins and inventory database updates)
- Creating cart objects (address autofill, tax calculation services, add to cart or checkout procedures)
- Third-party service providers (fraud services, authentication services)
- Plugins for websites
- Synchronous operations (such as processing orders and payments and updating inventory databases)

- Dynamic content, such as dynamic search and filters and recommendation engines

2. Virtual waiting rooms offer flexible & targeted protection

An additional feature that enables the current site is the virtual waiting room to function as if it were designed with heavy traffic in mind without requiring re-architecting.

All three of the issues with scaling lists are addressed by the solution:

- It automatically reroutes excessive traffic off the infrastructure, eliminating the need to forecast user behavior.
- It enables us to regulate the speed at which traffic enters the website, enabling the user to adjust traffic flow to your least scalable system's maximum throughput.
- Why Users who don't take the protected action never see the waiting room because it may be set up to protect the entire website, particular pages, or simply important bottlenecks like payment or login.

When traffic surpasses predetermined levels, virtual waiting rooms automatically reroute users to an online queue that resides off infrastructure. Visitors see a branded waiting area similar to the one below, complete with a progress meter, their queue number and an expected wait time. From here, they are returning to the location in a fair, regulated order at the pace they can control.

3.5.2 Best practices for performance and scaling for large workloads

Kubernetes features a multi-dimensional scale envelope, and the scale envelope with the workload changes based on the resources used. A cluster with 100 nodes and thousands of pods, or CRDs, could be a big example of this. In control plane terminology, a small cluster of resources can consist of 1,000 nodes, 1,000 pods, and other resources.

The success rate and latency of API server HTTP requests is the most indicative signal of scale of Kubernetes of a control plane since it is a proxy of control plane load.

1. AKS and Kubernetes scalability of the control plane

AKS A cluster is made up of a collection of nodes—either real or virtual machines (VMs)—that are controlled by the AKS-hosted Kubernetes control plane and that run Kubernetes agents. The upstream project limitations apply to AKS even if it improves the scalability and performance of the Kubernetes regulator smooth and its apparatuses.

The scope of scale of Kubernetes is multifaceted, with each resource type representing a dimension of the size. Resources differ from one another. For instance, watches are frequently set to secrets, which results in list requests to the Kube-apiserver, which adds to the expense and puts an excessively high strain on the control plane than when there are no watches.

All scaling of the resources in the cluster goes through the control plane hence the higher the scaling of the cluster in one dimension, the less the scaling in other dimensions. As an example, an AKS control plane limit is based on the number of pods that can be churned (mutated per second) in hundreds of thousands of pods in a cluster.

2. Kubernetes clients

Applications clients Applications clients are applications installed in the Kubernetes cluster that needs to be able to read or modify data by communicating with the Kube-api server objects. The behavior of these clients should be optimized in an effort to reduce the load the clients impose on the Kubernetes control plane as well as kube-api server. LIST requests may be costly. In dealing with lists, which may contain over a few hundred large items or over a few thousand small ones, you may find it well to bear the following in mind:

- When defining a new resource type (CRD), take into account how many objects (CRs) you anticipate someday existing.
- The size of the response is the main factor influencing the burden on the etcd and API server. These rules still hold true even if you filter the list using a field picker and only get a few results. The only exception is when metadata.name is used to retrieve a single object.
- If your code must keep an updated list of items in memory, try to avoid making repeated LIST calls. Alternatively, think about utilizing the Informer classes found in the majority of Kubernetes libraries. Informers effectively maintain an in-memory collection by automatically combining the LIST and WATCH functions.
- Read lengthy lists in sections if you are unable to use Informers or the API server cache.
- Don't listen more than is necessary. If you are unable to use Informers, think about how frequently the resources are listed in your application. Don't query the same list again right away after reading the last item in a lengthy list. Instead, you ought to hold off.
- Add appropriate exponential backoffs and retry policies to prevent clients from overwhelming the API server.
- Take into account how many instances of your client application are currently executing. The difference between having pods on each node performing the same task and having a single controller listing objects is substantial. Your solution won't scale to big clusters if you intend to have several instances of your client application that periodically list a lot of things.

3. Azure API and Platform throttling

A cloud application load can fluctuate with time depending on the quantity of people who are engaged or the types of activities that users can conduct. In case the demand of process required by the system is more than the available resources, then overloading can occur and there can be lack of performance and failures in the system.

To deal with the different loads of a cloud application you can just be able to give the program can access resources until a predetermined limit is reached, at which point it begins to throttle them. There are two tiers of throttling at Azure. Tenant and subscription queries are likewise throttled by ARM. If the request falls within the subscription and tenant throttling restrictions, ARM forwards it to the resource provider. Throttling limits that the resource provider uses are then derived based on its operations.

3.5.3 System scaling challenges in distributed systems

Data moves across several data centers when the company's system, application, or product expands internationally across several areas. This procedure may result in a slower system response time and an increase in network latency.

This primarily occurs as a result of the great distance between system data servers and the response delays caused by cross-region API calls. Therefore, as scalability increases, greater inter-service communication increasingly slows down the process.

Businesses frequently hire remote developers who specialize in optimizing distributed systems and lowering network latency issues in order to successfully manage scalability while controlling expenses.

- **Data Consistency vs. Availability Trade-offs**

In distributed systems, it is technically difficult to overcome the scaling challenge of simultaneously achieving great data availability and consistency. Strong consistency models cause system performance to lag, which ultimately results in certain clones using out-of-date data formats.

Database Scalability Bottlenecks

Monolithic databases that struggle under heavy read/write loads are one of the primary obstacles to database scalability, resulting in delayed queries and system outages. For instance, queries immediately slow down when inefficient indexes are used. Single-node databases become a major bottleneck due to inefficient read/write scaling patterns that overburden the core database.

Increased System Complexity

As a system expands, its management gets increasingly complicated. All of the aforementioned elements are involved in maintaining APIs and the overall system architecture.

1. Managing system failures and recovery is essential since system growth increases dependencies and failure spots.
2. Distributed logs will provide difficulties with debugging and tracing, as well as issues with observation, security, and data protection.
3. Costs, monitoring problems, and unmanageable manual scaling techniques.

Multiple-Choice Questions (MCQs)

1. **What is the primary role of Ingress in Kubernetes?**

   A) To expose Pods only within the cluster
   B) To manage external access to services, usually HTTP/HTTPS
   C) To allocate persistent storage to containers
   D) To schedule Pods across nodes

2. **Which Kubernetes object is mainly used for internal load balancing and service discovery?**

   A) Namespace
   B) ReplicaSet
   C) Service
   D) ConfigMap

3. **What is the purpose of a CNI plugin in Kubernetes?**

   A) To manage storage volumes
   B) To provide networking capabilities for Pods
   C) To handle application logging
   D) To configure container images

4. **Which of the following is an example of a commonly used Kubernetes CNI plugin?**

   A) Helm
   B) Prometheus
   C) Calico
   D) Grafana

5. **In Kubernetes, what does egress traffic refer to?**

   A) Traffic entering the cluster from outside
   B) Traffic leaving a Pod or cluster to external destinations
   C) Traffic only between worker nodes
   D) Traffic only between containers in the same Pod

6. Which component enables Kubernetes to use external storage systems in a standardized way?

A) CRI
B) CSI
C) CNI
D) API Server

7. Which type of Kubernetes storage remains available even after a Pod is deleted?

A) EmptyDir
B) HostPath
C) Persistent Volume
D) Container filesystem

8. What is a major challenge in Kubernetes networking at scale?

A) Lack of container runtimes
B) Increased latency and network policy complexity
C) Inability to run multiple Pods
D) Absence of cluster monitoring tools

9. Which Kubernetes feature helps distribute incoming traffic across multiple Pods?

A) StatefulSet
B) DaemonSet
C) Service Load Balancing
D) Secret

10. Why is persistent storage important in large-scale Kubernetes deployments?

A) It reduces the need for Pods
B) It ensures data survives Pod restarts and rescheduling
C) It replaces networking components
D) It improves only CPU performance

Answer

1	2	3	4	5	6	7	8	9	10
B	C	B	C	B	B	C	B	C	B

Chapter 4

Observability And Debugging Distributed Kubernetes Systems

4.1 Limitations of traditional monitoring

The current Kubernetes infrastructures are not similar to the static and monolithic structure that traditional monitoring tools were initially intended to monitor. In the previous architectures applications were executed on a few long-lived servers, network paths were deterministic and system components were rarely modified. In these types of environments, monitoring was predominantly based on host-level measurements (CPU, memory, disc I/O, and network utilization throughout) . This was quite effective when infrastructure was fairly stable and application boundaries are well defined.

Nevertheless, the systems based on Kubernetes also provide a very dynamic and distributed model of operation. Containers are randomly created and destroyed, pods are restarted automatically, nodes are able to either join or leave clusters and workloads are scaled horizontally based on demand. Services are communicating using overlay networks, typically over multiple clusters and cloud regions. In this regard, conventional monitoring tools are not suited to the change pace. Systems where topology, traffic patterns and service dependencies keep changing do not support the use of static dashboards and threshold-driven alerts.

The other constraining factor is visibility. Conventional monitoring usually measures the infrastructure components individually (servers, virtual machines, network devices) instead of measuring the service-level behavior and the end-to-end request flows. Kubernetes also has reliability built on the health of the nodes, as well as on the interactions among the microservices, and the components of the control plane, the layers of the network, and the storage subsystems. It can lead to fragmented information and to complex analyses of the underlying causes since it is difficult to keep such a process track without a contextual understanding of such relations, which will be time-consuming.

Finally, the traditional approaches to monitoring often assume the possibility of failure and degradation as linear and predictable. Systems based on the cloud, in contrast, are said to exhibit emergent behavior, such as cascading failures, and retry storms, as well as namespace resource contention and control plane bottlenecks. These trends require observability strategies that emphasize correlation, causality and distributed tracing as compared to single metric collection. The gap between the conventional monitoring properties and the new cloud-native operational demands expands in proportion to the size of Kubernetes environment.

4.1.1 Infrastructure-Centric Monitoring in a Service-Oriented Architecture

Traditional monitoring systems were designed on monolithic usage and were implemented on long-lived servers that were stable. Operation visibility in these types of environments was centred on infrastructure health which included load on the CPU, memory, disc I/O, and network throughput. The basic premise was simple: as long as the server was healthy and available, the application that was hosted on it would work properly. Stability of a machine was thus equated to reliability.

Service-Oriented Architecture (SOA) was a fundamental challenge of this assumption. As opposed to one tightly coupled application, there is a decomposition of functionality in autonomous services that interact at the network. They each can be independent, scale, and evolve at different rates, and run on independent hosts. According to this model, the reliability ceases to depend on the health of individual machines and is now based on the correctness and performance of interactions between services. The infrastructure-focused monitoring that monitors systems at the host level is out of synergy with the service-oriented system architecture.

1. Host Health Does Not Guarantee Service Health

Infrastructure metrics in a service-based environment only give partial information. One node can be reporting normal CPU and memory usage when the service on it is having high and excessive latency, misconfigurations, dependency timeouts or partial logic failures.

Infrastructure monitoring typically measures:

- Resource consumption
- Process availability
- Basic connectivity

However, service reliability depends on:

- Response time consistency
- Error rate behavior
- Transaction success ratios
- Downstream dependency performance

It is thus possible to have a system which is healthy on infrastructure view but has users with poor performance. This detachment shows one of the fundamental drawbacks of infrastructure-based monitoring: it monitors the state of resources and not service behavior.

2. Cascading Failures and Dependency Blindness

Service oriented systems are by definition interconnected. One client request is likely to pass through several services before it is completed. New dynamics of failure are added by these dependency chains.

Take a case whereby downstream authentication service is slowed down by latency spikes. Upstream services can start to resend requests and overload and drain connection pools. In the long run, such a stress spreads over the system even to what were initially healthy components. Distributed architectures are typified by such cascading failures.

Traditional monitoring tools which are based on isolated hosts do not have a view of such inter-service relationships. They might not be able to realize large levels of resource consumption before the cascade has advanced far. In the absence of contextual identity of dependency graphs and interactions of services, root causes are complicated and time-consuming to determine.

3. Distributed and Dynamic Execution Environments

SOA environments are frequently distributed across various data centers, cloud regions and disparate technology stack. Services can be implemented in various programming languages, and they can be deployed in various platforms as well as be linked with different communication protocols. Each host monitored separately creates piecemeal signals that are not inherently reassembled to create request flows across the end-to-end.

This complexity increases in Kubernetes based systems. The containers are short lived, pods are dynamically scheduled and workloads are horizontally scaled based on demand. Instances of services can be offered and clustered on a high frequency and can move the execution amongst nodes. Monitoring tools, such as infrastructure-centric tools, where host identities are stable, and configurations remain fixed, find it difficult to maintain continuity in that environment.

An increase in resource consumption can be a sign of healthy scaling as opposed to failure. On the other hand, a severe service degradation can take place without observable infrastructure stress. The impractical thresholds that are imposed on dynamic systems also tend to produce too much noise or too little alert.

4. Architectural Implication

Infrastructure-based monitoring is an indication of an architectural worldview where machines are considered to be the main unit of reliability. With service orientated systems that are based on Kubernetes however, the actual unit of reliability is the service and its interaction network.

Ensuring uptime in such environments requires visibility into:

- Service-level latency and error propagation
- Dependency relationships and communication patterns
- Distributed request flows across components

The detriment of the conventional monitoring is not only technical but conceptual in nature. It was intended to fit another period of architecture. With the change of systems towards a distributed, elastic and service-focused approach, monitoring strategies have to shift towards observing the infrastructure, to understanding the system as a whole.

4.1.2 Challenges in Observing Ephemeral and Elastic Workloads

The tools used in traditional IT operations monitoring are designed to keep an eye on infrastructure and static entities for signals known as the "three pillars" (logs, metrics, and traces). These signals are routinely gathered from several manageable hosts running monolithic applications. For very good reasons, the corresponding apps in today's cloud-native environment have been divided among platforms like

Kubernetes and atomized into containerized microservices. Kubernetes is a crucial technological and architectural option for today's modern apps because of its scalability and self-managing resilience.

The flexibility of Kubernetes' resource-based modelling is one of its main advantages. It is not a set of imperative directives, but rather a declarative approach. One of Kubernetes' controllers spins up a pod with those features when you design a Kubernetes pod that wraps containers with particular attributes and create a manifest. Kubernetes takes care of the necessary processes, so the user doesn't have to worry about the specifics of getting to the pod in its final state. The Kubernetes API is used to manage resources, always using a desire-intent versus reality comparison approach. Kubernetes continuously verifies that the resources that are available match the intended resources.

However, when it comes to monitoring these same deployments, the same advantages of running apps on Kubernetes might provide a significant challenge. Let's examine some of the most significant obstacles.

- **Dynamic and Ephemeral Environment**

Infrastructure in Kubernetes is predetermined and unchangeable. It is advised to just launch a new pod with a new name if there is a problem with an incorrectly configured pod or if something has to be upgraded. There is no simple way to upgrade the current pod. The same holds true for the pod's internal containers. These restart when necessary, making it difficult to monitor and much more difficult to debug the performance of the infrastructure supporting your apps.

- **A New Meaning for Scale**

Scale has a new meaning due to the proliferation of microservices. In old production systems, 20,000 physical servers or "virtual machines" (VMs) were reserved for the enterprise end of the scale. However, in the Kubernetes world, one person can simply deploy and orchestrate 30,000 pods using a single cluster. In theory, Kubernetes clusters might have up to 150,000 pods.

Each container can add an extra 20 metrics, and a single pod can readily disclose 25 distinct metrics. You can get an estimate of how many signals could be produced at one time by multiplying these numbers by 30,000.

Additionally, to comprehend the size of data sets that must be managed for ingesting, storage, and analysis of Kubernetes observability data, scale the preceding results by a typical scraping frequency of 10 seconds.

Distributed Nature of Kubernetes Components

Kubernetes is a distributed system made up of various parts operating on several nodes, which can be either physical or virtual. Although many of them may be accessed via the Kubernetes API server, the observer must perform this duty because there is no correlation between all of the signals that are exposed.

The Kubernetes API's metrics and signals are unprocessed and difficult to interpret. To turn the data into visualizations using Kubernetes-centric dashboards and log analysis tools that can identify patterns and comprehend trends, an additional layer of analysis is required.

Distributed Nature of Kubernetes Monitoring Data

Reducing the time it takes to identify and fix problems depends on having the proper context, at the right time, and in the appropriate location. The problem is that this data is dispersed across vertical silos (e.g., a log collection focused tool, a metrics monitoring focused tool, an APM solution), which makes it challenging and time-consuming for SREs to create a broad enough picture to comprehend what is going on and what needs to be done about it. Once more, a platform that can aggregate all of this Kubernetes telemetry data is the best option given the volume of signals and dispersed monitoring data.

Understanding Kubernetes Signals

Lack of knowledge about Kubernetes' internal workings is one of the main issues that organizations face. Acquiring and displaying signals is insufficient, and while a thorough grasp of Kubernetes is possible, one could contend that Kubernetes monitoring solutions should take the lead in connecting seemingly unrelated signals, giving users answers rather than simply raw data. Because Kubernetes can run and fix a lot of performance issues (self-managing), administrators may find it difficult when more complex issues require manual intervention and inquiry.

4.1.3 Absence of Distributed Context and Dependency Awareness

The capacity to determine a system's current status from the data it generates, primarily logs, metrics, and traces, is known as observability. These signals help you observe what's going on inside your system, not just whether it's up or down, rather than treating it like a black box.

In simple words, observability helps you understand your system from the outside. When something goes wrong, you can quickly see what changed, which part of the system is affected, and how different components are interacting.

- **The Evolution from Monitoring to Observability**

Traditional monitoring was designed for simpler systems. You defined a predetermined set of measures, created dashboards and waited until alarms started going off. This was effective when systems were foreseeable and in case of failure it was easy to detect. This method began to disintegrate as architectures became more complicated. In case a problem did not correspond to a prebuilt alert, then monitoring would only inform you that something was amiss, not what.

As an example, CPU and memory may be fine, but users are reporting slow page loads or not being able to checkout.

This was further complicated by microservices. One user request can use an API gateway, multiple backend services, a message queue, a database, and a third-pazrty API. Failure to speed up one downstream dependency can lead to mistakes elsewhere in a completely new place.

In this world it is not sufficient to know that a service is up, but rather the flow of requests within the system and the dependency of services on each other.

It is this gap that motivated the change of reactive monitoring to exploratory observability.

Observability allows new questions to be answered in case of something unforeseen, rather than making use of some predefined checks. Whenever an alert is set off, you may trace the request route, locate where latency was added, and know which service or dependency introduced the problem.

Static Dashboards vs. Dynamic Exploration

Statically displayed dashboards present you with what you had previously anticipated to view. They are familiar with familiar problems such as a server running out of disk space but are not familiar with unfamiliar or complex problems. In cases where something unusual occurs, such dashboards may create more questions than answers.

Monitors you on dynamic exploration. Rather than viewing pre-recorded graphs, you can peek at real-time data, filter by user, area, or request, and visually follow a problem through services in real-time. The need to guess is minimized, discovery is more appropriate, and such is what the modern, distributed systems require.

Traces and Dependency Awareness

Traces provide the route of a request as it traverses several services. They assist with the interaction of the various components and where the latency or failures lie.

As an example, when an API request is slower than it should, tracing will allow you to understand what service or database call slowed down. This renders the process of root cause identification in complicated, distributed systems significantly quicker.

- **Why Observability Matters for Modern Architectures**

Contemporary applications are no longer single-service-based, but rather a multi-service, multi-platform, and multi-environs application.

With microservices, one user request can easily go through numerous services. A ripple effect may happen when one service slows down or fails in the system. Observability assists you in drawing dependencies among services, bottlenecks, and locating failures and making rapid isolations without affecting other unrelated systems.

Kubernetes has brought about dynamic scaling, self-healing, and ephemeral workloads, and therefore powerful and more difficult to monitor. It is possible to create, terminate, or re-schedule pods and containers on any node. Services can be portable, can be scaled and rely on various underlying resources.

Observability in Kubernetes enables you to monitor the behaviour of the system in real-time and know how the workloads interact and measure the effects of scaling events or resource constraints.

Observability provides you with profound sight into dependencies, failure points, and changes impact by enabling you to operate modern and distributed frameworks reliably and react to problems swiftly prior to them influencing consumers.

4.1.4 Operational Noise and Threshold-Based Alerting in Traditional Monitoring

The alert noise is indicated as non-actionable, repetitive, or low impact warnings that distract the teams against real events. The aim of alert noise reduction is to improve the quality of the signal and not to reduce the alert volume. Overwhelming noise is the cause of operational risk, fatigue of alert, and slow response to an incident. The common reasons are static thresholds, duplicate alarms, poor severity classification, and absence of correlation.

The current IT environments are loud. Microservice, hybrid clouds and containerised applications produce an astonishing quantity of telemetry information per second. This information is essential for IT operations, NOC teams, and Site Reliability Engineers (SREs), but only if it can be put to use. Everything turns into background noise when things aren't like this. We may experience an alert noise issue if your staff is more likely to ignore messages than to deal with the issues they are facing.

This is an operational danger rather than merely an annoyance. Long response times and potential outages occur from signals that could be crucial being buried beneath floods of low-priority alerts.

Alert Noise

Any message that diverts an operator from crucial activities without offering actionable value is referred to as alert noise in the context of IT operations. As a result, it opposes the discrepancy between the total alert volumes (produced by your monitoring systems) and those that require human intervention.

An example of a typical alarm sounds could be:

- **Repetitive Alerts:** One minute in and one minute out, the same thing is brought back until something positive is claimed to have been accomplished.
- **Low-Impact Threshold Breaches:** notifications for measurements that are somewhat out of boundaries but do not affect "service level agreements" (SLAs) or user experience.
- **Cascading Alerts:** A "storm" of warnings for a single underlying cause occurs when one of the essential components (such an underlying database) fails and each dependant application creates a separate alert.

- **False Positives:** Alerts generated during brief network outages or improperly configured sensors that did not show the presence of a real problem.

Alert noise is becoming an increasingly difficult challenge to manage as infrastructure complexity increases. Without action, the cacophony quickly surpasses the human body's ability to react since it grows linearly with the infrastructure.

Common Sources of Alert Noise

1. **Static Thresholds**: Normal variance is ignored by these fixed numbers, such as "Alert if latency > 200ms." Innovative traffic patterns during peak hours or batch processing tasks can generate a great deal of noise and set static thresholds without reporting a problem.

2. **Infrastructure-centric alerts without service context**: Raw infrastructure metrics alerts, such as high disk usage on a certain node, frequently don't provide context. The signal is irrelevant if the node is part of a self-healing cluster, which automatically spins up a replacement. One of the main causes of the noise is alerts that deny the correct state of the actual service.

3. **Duplicate Alerts in Dependent Systems**: One service is closely connected to another in microservices architectures. The frontend app, inventory service, and checkout service may all fail health checks in the event of a payment gateway failure. This would result in three or four different notifications of an event for a single incident in nonreciprocal relationships.

4. **Lack of Correlation**: Similar to dependence issues, events are handled independently in the absence of correlation. 50 separate servers may receive "server unreachable" alerts in the event of a network switch failure. There is no method to control the noise level if this data cannot be linked to a single "switch down."

5. **Poor Severity Classification**: The goal with severity levels is defeated when all alerts are classified as "critical" or high-grade. Engineers are unable to prioritise the system if a disk's 80% maximum capacity creates the same level of urgency for a site-wide outage. Misclassification creates both urgent and informative data noise.

Static alert thresholds can cause noise in dynamic Kubernetes environments. Viewing metrics, logs and traces in silos limits diagnostic capabilities. Use platforms that correlate these signals so you can see, for example, how a spike in pod CPU usage correlates with error rates or trace latency. This holistic view propels faster issue identification and resolution.

4.2 Metrics, logs, and distributed tracing

The systems of modern Kubernetes are highly dynamic and distributed environments that have application components decoupled, scaled independently and regularly rescheduled across nodes. The visibility on infrastructure level is not adequate in such architectures to understand the behavior of systems. Reliability is based on the interpretation of many layers of telemetry representing performance, state transitions and service interactions in real time.

Cloud-native workloads create constant data streams of operational data. Failures in distributed systems follow non-linear, complex, patterns of failure unlike monolithic systems where failures were usually local and predictable. Single-dimensional monitoring is not capable of diagnosing latency propagation, retry storms, intermittent dependency failures, and bottlenecks at the control-plane. Total transparency demands organized telemetry that has the ability to record the system trends and finer details of execution.

The pillars that constitute the basic telemetry that are used to observe Kubernetes environments are metrics, logs, and distributed tracing. The different types of signals have different views on the behavior of the systems. Combining them, they allow the engineers not to operate on the surface but observe their operations on a deeper level, respond to incidents much quicker, and analyze roots of error more accurately.

As clusters grow and systems of micro services multiply, the need to correlate these signals grows exponentially. The distributed systems with non-cohesive telemetry turn opaque and reliability engineering turns into a reactive and inefficient process. Good observability starts with the realization of the complementary nature of metrics, logs and tracing.

4.2.1 Metrics: Quantitative Measurement of System Behavior

Metrics are numerical values that demonstrate a system's performance over time. A collection of properties, such as name, value, label, and date, are part of the default structure of metrics, which makes querying quicker and simpler and optimises storage so you may store them longer.

Key performance indicators, such as CPU and memory consumption, error rate, network latency, and anything else that provides information about the condition and functionality of your system, are typically called metrics. Response time, peak load, and the quantity of HTTP requests fulfilled are some KPIs that can be monitored when keeping an eye on a website.

Metrics can be used to determine the severity of an issue, offer insight and visibility, and set off warnings when certain characteristics surpass a certain level. Teams can assess system performance and seriousness with the help of these indicators. For example, you observe an abrupt increase in the system's traffic while keeping an eye on the website's service requests per second. Metrics can provide an explanation for the spike, which may be the result of malicious activity, improper service configuration, or design flaws. hence aiding in the problem's discovery and evaluation.

Benefits of Metrics

Metrics mainly help alert the DevOps and other teams of any possible errors.

- **Business execution:** Because metrics are numerical and don't place a significant strain on the system, they are simple to maintain and query. They are therefore excellent for historical data displays, particularly for real-time KPI monitoring and long-term data analysis for trends.
- **Lower cost:** Since the cost of metrics does not increase with the number of users or other system activity that produces a lot of data, they are more economical than logs.
- **Fast processing despite increased storage:** When application traffic increases, logs increase disc utilisation, processing complexity, visualisation speed, and operating expenses; metrics do not. Metric traffic can be prevented from increasing at the same rate as user traffic by using client-side aggregation.
- **Alerts:** Because executing queries against an in-memory, time-series database is more effective, dependable, and economical than running queries against a distributed system and then adding up the results to determine whether an alert should be sent, metrics are preferable for sending alerts.
- **System health performance insight:** Metrics can measure system performance over time and offer insightful information, including changes that can be put into practice. It also offers alerts for real-time system monitoring. For instance, when the system is overcrowded or unavailable, etc. Additionally, it can identify abnormalities and establish new benchmarks for future objectives.

Limitations of Metrics

Metrics have constraints of their own, just like the other observability pillars. Here are a few of them:

- **System scoped:** It is challenging to ascertain what is occurring outside of a system since application logs and metrics are system-scoped. Request scoping metrics is another option, but it necessitates more label dispersion, which increases the amount of metric storage.
- **High cardinality slows performance:** One user identification is high cardinality data in a system with thousands or millions of users. High cardinality data can slow down your monitoring tools and make it more difficult to query. There could be hundreds of possible permutations for monitoring tags with high cardinality. The amount of processing power and storage required to store all the data could make the system expensive.
- **Multi-format data storage:** Because a wide range of data and analysis techniques are needed, using metrics can be difficult. Another issue is how to keep data that has been gathered from different sources and in different formats.
- **Limited diagnosis capabilities:** Diagnosing an incident with just measurements is difficult. For instance, it is challenging to aggregate metrics by tags, filter tags, and repeat the filtering process in a real-world scenario where a tag may have hundreds of values. Additionally, the cardinality of your data set is greatly increased by adding tags.

4.2.2 Logs: Structured Event Records and Diagnostic Context

It is not easy to diagnose an incident using only measurements. An example is that, in a realistic scenario where a tag can contain hundreds of values, it is difficult to aggregate metrics by tags, to filter tags and repeat the process of filtering. Additionally, the cardinality of your data set is greatly increased by adding tags.

Because JSON is widely supported and easy to read by humans, it is the most used format for structured logs. There are other formats, like as XML, although they are less used in contemporary logging stacks.

A typical, unstructured log entry would be a straightforward text line indicating that a user's login attempt failed and providing an explanation. The machine would need complex parsing rules, but a human being would be able to understand this. Or now think of its more formal equivalent: a JSON object with individual fields of "timestamp," "level," "message," "event-type," "user-id," "reason" and "source-ip.

This structure of log is more feasible at the initial stage. Any USER_LOGIN_FAIL events, any events involving a particular user ID or just any debug message sent by a particular IP address can easily be queried. The inherent advantage of organized logging is its ability to process logs as data sets.

Key Benefits of Adopting Structured Logs

- **Better Search and Querying:** When such fields as user-id, transaction-id or error-code are specifically given, it is possible to run exact queries. Just imagine that you can find any logs of a particular customer experiencing issues fast, or that you can find all the cases of a particular error code across all of your microservices. This saves a lot of time that will be wasted in trying to sort out useless log lines.
- **Improved Performance and Efficiency**: Log management systems have the capability of ingesting, indexing and analysing structured data much more efficiently than unstructured text. Since data can be better compacted and managed, this contributes to faster search results, reduced processing cost, and decreased storage expenses.
- **Consistency Across Systems:** Consistency of log structure is required in a complex system where there are many services, applications, and infrastructure. It allows a centralised view of log aggregation and analysis that provides you with a unified picture about the behaviour of the entire system.

- **Eases Automation:** Machines can read logs which are automation friendly. You may build automated alerts on selected field values or pattern of logs (e.g. alert when error rate of payment service has hit a threshold). Also, structured logs can be easily integrated with CI/CD pipelines through rollback triggers or automated quality gates.
- **Improved Analytics and Business Intelligence:** Organized data regarding log can be sent to analytics systems to obtain information about user behaviour, adoption of features, trends in performance, and other indicators that are relevant to business on top of troubleshooting.
- **Easy Debugging and Troubleshooting:** Structured logs provide effective context on a problem occurrence. It is considerably simpler to identify the underlying cause of an issue when you receive related metadata, such as request IDs, session IDs, and program versions, rather than just an error message.

4.2.3 Distributed Tracing: End-to-End Request Flow Visibility

Google's Dapper paper from 2010 served as the foundation for distributed tracing. By having each service emit information about the actions it accomplished and enhance those signals with a common identity, the aim is to indirectly watch how a group of services interact with one another.

We refer to those individual signals as "spans," and they often have a unique identity and a descriptive name. A "trace," which is made up of n spans, includes a single span. Every span can have an infinite number of children.

As long as the trace ID is maintained and subsequent spans carry it, this data paradigm ensures that a trace can be continued. For this method to function, each service must transmit this correlation information to the subsequent downstream service.

Consider each of your own application services or the platform's components as a potential source of such a span in the context of Kubernetes. Following the trail of spans produced by those components and examining the metadata, like as duration or Kubernetes-related properties, will then help you understand how an application operates.

You may track a particular request's performance while it interacts with hundreds of other services by using a unique identifier (the trace ID). Because of this, distributed tracing is essential to a Kubernetes observability approach for the entire cluster. In the existing complicated cloud infrastructure, it is the most reliable way to learn about the group of loosely connected services that make up an application.

Despite its apparent simplicity, distributed tracing offers useful details about your Kubernetes cluster. Here are a few instances of the possible advantages:

- **End-to-end visibility.** Distributed tracing technologies are used by developers and operators to track how user requests interact with other microservices. DevOps teams may readily monitor performance, throughput, functionality, and infrastructure bottlenecks by using GPS navigation and coordinates to do a retrospective of each point on the map.
- **Service dependencies.** To find any dependencies and interactions between various services, you should employ distributed tracing.
- **Anomaly detection.** To quickly identify anomalies that affect application performance, use healthy traces as a comparison.
- **Enhanced application debugging.** For debugging and troubleshooting applications, use distributed tracing tools along with cluster logs and analytics.

4.3 Control Plane Observability

In Kubernetes architectures, the control plane is the cluster's brain. While the majority of observability capabilities are focused on the data plane and application workloads, performance, the control plane stability and responsiveness is also of paramount importance to the reliability of the system in general. When the control plane becomes compromised, the behavior of the whole cluster becomes unrealistic, with the slowing of the schedules, stalling of scaling, hanging deployments, and broken self-healing.

The Kubernetes control plane is an implementation of a number of interacting components: the API server, the scheduler, the controller manager and the underlying state store. These components synchronize cluster state, impose desired configurations, and control workload lifecycle. In contrast to the application services, the control plane failures do not always reflect in the crash of the applications but rather in the latency increments, delays in the reconciliation process, or inconsistency of the cluster state.

The observability at the control plane layer demands the visibility of the coordination mechanisms, as opposed to business logic. Performance metrics like API request latency, etcd performance, scheduling throughput and controller reconciliation loops will give information on systemic health. Lacking the ability to monitor these signals, reliability engineering will be incomplete, with much of the large-scale Kubernetes accidents being caused by bottlenecks in the control plane instead of defects in the applications.

The control plane has a heavy load as the clusters grow in size in terms of nodes, namespaces and multi-cluster topologies. Control plane components can be overwhelmed by high object churn, too many watch connections or a poor design custom controller. Thus, to design trustworthy cloud-native systems, observability of the control plane should be treated as the first-order issue.

4.3.1 API Server Performance and Request Latency

The Kubernetes API is made available by the API server (kube-apiserver), a front-end part of the Kubernetes control plane. The sole component that communicates directly with etcd is the API Server, which is in charge of all activities pertaining to the distributed storage component etcd datastore. A single REST API is used for communication amongst all other components. Using a list-watch API, Controller Manager, Scheduler, Kube proxy, and Kubelet keep an eye on resource changes and respond appropriately.

By keeping an eye on the kube-apiserver metrics, you may find and fix delays and problems and verify that the service is functioning as intended.

The requests to apiserver, their origin, the action they take, and their success may all be tracked using the counter vector apiserver_request_total.

Additionally, the Read Request Success Rate and Write Request Success Rate are available:

Verify the Request Success Rate

sum(irate(apiserver_request_total{code=~"20.*",verb=~"GET|LIST"} [5m]))/sum(irate(apiserver_request_total{verb=~"GET|LIST"} [5m]))

Write the Success Rate of the Request

sum (irate (apiserver_request_total{code=~"20. *", verb! ~"GET|LIST|WATCH|CONNECT"} [5m]))/sum (irate (apiserver_request_total{verb! ~"GET|LIST|WATCH|CONNECT"} [5m]))

Additionally, a histogram vector of apiserver_request_duration_seconds_bucket is exposed by kube-apiserver. This metric is used to compute the time in seconds taken by each request of the Kubernetes API server. A histogram_quantile can be used to visualize the distribution of delay amongst verbs.

Process_cpu_seconds_total, which measures the total CPU time spent by users and the system in seconds, is another crucial metric. To find out how many CPU seconds apiserver, kube-controller-manager, etcd, and scheduler use, use PromQL.

Admission controller latency must also be taken into account. Requests to the Kubernetes API server are intercepted by the admission controller after they have been verified and approved, but before the object is made persistent. To obtain admission and webhook latency metrics, Kube-apiserver exposes histogram vectors of apiserver_admission_controller_admission_duration_seconds_bucket.

Kubernetes configuration, state, and metadata data are stored in the etcd cluster. A histogram vector of etcd_request_duration_seconds_bucket is exposed by the kube-apiserver, which tracks the latency of API requests between kube-apiserver and etcd. The latency increases when creating multiple Deployments in parallel.

Key elements of Kubernetes are the kube-controller-manager, kube-scheduler, and kubelet. These elements are clients using the LIST/WATCH technique to communicate with API servers. The delay or time in seconds for calls to the API server is measured by the metric rest_client_request_duration_seconds_bucket. It is a useful method to keep an eye on the communications between the API and the kube-controller-manager, kubelet, or scheduler, and to see if these requests are being answered in a timely manner.

Requests received directly from Kubernetes components and other clients are included in apiserver_request_total, which is the total amount of requests handled by all apiservers. The amount of queries submitted to the apiserver through a REST client is called rest_client_requests_total, and it is labelled by the http method and other client-specific characteristics.

4.3.2 Scheduler Throughput and Pod Placement Efficiency

The Kubernetes, the control plane is the cluster's brain architectures. Although most observability capabilities are dedicated to the application workloads and the data plane performance, the control plane stability and responsiveness is also of paramount importance to the reliability of the system in general. When the control plane becomes compromised, the behavior of the whole cluster becomes unrealistic, with the slowing of the schedules, stalling of scaling, hanging deployments, and broken self-healing.

The Kubernetes control plane is an implementation of a number of interacting components: the API server, the scheduler, the controller manager and the underlying state store. These components synchronize cluster state, impose desired configurations, and control workload lifecycle. In contrast to the application services, the control plane failures do not always reflect in the crash of the applications but rather in the latency increments, delays in the reconciliation process, or inconsistency of the cluster state.

The observability at the control plane layer demands the visibility of the coordination mechanisms, as opposed to business logic. Performance metrics like API request latency, etcd performance, scheduling throughput and controller reconciliation loops will give information on systemic health. Lacking the ability to monitor these signals, reliability engineering will be incomplete, with much of the large-scale Kubernetes accidents being caused by bottlenecks in the control plane instead of defects in the applications.

The control plane has a heavy load as the clusters grow in size in terms of nodes, namespaces and multi-cluster topologies. Control plane components can be overwhelmed by high object churn, too many watch connections or a poor design custom controller. Thus, to design trustworthy cloud-native systems, observability of the control plane should be treated as the first-order issue.

4.3.3 Controller Reconciliation Loops and Cluster State Consistency

The controllers in Kubernetes are run as a continuous control loop model that ensures the difference between the desired state that is specified by the user and the observed state in the cluster is kept. This process is referred to as the reconciliation loop and it is the core of Kubernetes reliability. Controllers are constantly updating the state of the cluster, detect drift, and take corrective measures to restore the state instead of performing tasks only once.

The main component of this process is the Kubernetes API server which stores the desired state in etcd. Controllers do not directly touch the infrastructure, rather, they communicate with the API server and are based on the intentional declaration. The system is thus pushed by comparison of states as opposed to imperative enforcing.

The Reconciliation Loop Model

Each controller follows a structured cycle:

- Observe the current state of relevant resources using watch APIs and shared informers.
- Compare the observed state with the desired specification stored in the API server.
- Determine corrective actions required to close any state gap.
- Act by creating, updating, or deleting resources.
- Requeue, if necessary, especially in cases of transient failures.

Controllers are designed to be idempotent, meaning repeated reconciliation attempts produce the same stable result. This ensures safe retries and consistent convergence.

Event-Driven Architecture and Work Queues

Controllers rely on:

- Watch API streams to receive real-time updates about resource changes.
- Shared informers to maintain cached resource state and reduce API server load.
- Work queues to process reconciliation tasks asynchronously.

As a resource alters, e.g. Pod is deleted or there is replica mismatch, the controller inserts a key to its work queue. The event-based model will avoid continuous polling and be more scalable. Nevertheless, with an increase in queue depth, or a slowdown in the processing speed, the reconciliation latency increases which may delay convergence of the state.

Ensuring Cluster State Consistency

Cluster consistency depends on how efficiently controllers process reconciliation tasks. In high-churn environments—such as rolling deployments, autoscaling spikes, or node failures—the number of events can increase dramatically. If reconciliation cannot keep pace:

- Replica counts may temporarily drift
- Failed Pods may take longer to recover
- Rollouts may stall
- Autoscaling actions may lag

Monitoring reconciliation duration and work queue backlog provides early warning of control plane saturation.

kube-controller-manager and Multi-Controller Dynamics

The kube-controller-manager runs multiple controllers within a single process, including:

- Deployment controller
- Replica Set controller
- Node controller
- Job controller
- Endpoint Slice controller

Each controller maintains independent reconciliation logic and queue processing. Contention for CPU or API server bandwidth within the controller manager can affect overall cluster stability.

Reconciliation and Eventual Consistency

Kubernetes works on an eventual consistency. The system does not assure the instant convergence but only that in the long run, there is the coincidence of the actual state with the stated desired state. The pace at which this convergence occurs is a very important measure of reliability.

Good observability of the reconciliation loops (observing the queue depth, error rates, requeuing frequency, and latency to reconcile) gives an insight into the speed with which the cluster is able to correct drift following failures or modifications. In order to guarantee reliability, elasticity, and control plane resiliency within large-scale Kubernetes setup, one has to maintain a healthy performance of the reconciliation procedure.

4.3.4 ETCD Health and Distributed State Management

Deterministic consensus is needed to coordinate state at distributed nodes. In its absence, systems degenerate into write contests, stale reads and split-brain errors. etcd attempts to address the problem by becoming a strongly consistent, Raft consensus is the basis of this distributed key-value store.

etcd uses replicated commits with leader election and quorum-based commits. A write is not recognized until it has been persisted by a majority of the members of the cluster, which ensures linearizable integrity. This renders etcd appropriate in storing important cluster state as accuracy is valued more than bare throughput.

In Kubernetes, the authority data store is etcd. All control plane components maintain desirable and observed state to etcd. Etcd achieves the consistency guarantees required to support large-scale container workloads and recover predictively in the face of failures by ensuring these state transitions are agreed upon by all nodes before commit.

Quorum and Distributed Architecture.

An etcd deployment is made of several members (usually 3 or 5). Full copy of the keyspace is stored by each member and each member is involved into consensus. The cluster will keep on serving reads and writes provided that a majority (quorum) of the members are reachable. Failure of minorities has no negative effects on durability and consistency. But in case of quorum loss, writes are stalled so as to maintain correctness.

Raft enjoys members in one leader and many followers:

- All writes go through the leader.
- The leader appends updates to its replicated log.
- Followers receive and persist the log entries.
- A write is committed only after acknowledgment from a majority.

Raft's election procedure automatically elects a new leader in the event that the current one fails, guaranteeing that there is only one active leader at a time.

Strong Consistency and Control Plane Guarantees

etcd supports linearized reads and writes. A successful write implies that it has been permanently endured by a majority. Linearizable reads are used to ensure that the clients see the most recent committed state.

In the case of Kubernetes, it ensures:

- Controllers reconcile against accurate cluster state.
- The scheduler makes placement decisions based on current data.
- Control-plane components do not diverge on resource truth.

Because the only part that interacts directly with etcd is the API server, all state mutations pass through authentication, authorization, and admission before being committed.

Watch API and Event-Driven State Propagation

etcd provides a watch API, which broadcasts key changes to clients. Consumers subscribe to important prefixes rather than polling, and get real-time notification.

Kubernetes is based on this primitive, constructing its reconciliation model:

- Controllers watch resource changes.
- Updates in etcd propagate through the API server.
- Controllers react and drive the system toward desired state.

This event-driven model reduces latency and avoids unnecessary load from polling.

Performance Sensitivity and Operational Health

etcd is very sensitive to disk and network latency.

Disk I/O:

Write-Ahead Log (WAL) has to commit on each write. Long WAL fsync time has a direct proportional relationship with commit latency, and may lead to high request latency at the API server and propagating delays during reconciliation.

Network latency:

The consensus needs a two-way communication between the leader and the followers. Increased peer latency reduces the commit throughput and may cause unwanted elections.

The important indicators of operation are:

- Leader election frequency
- WAL fsync duration
- Backend commit duration
- Peer round-trip latency
- Database size and compaction metrics

Frequent leader changes or elevated commit latency indicate instability that directly impacts control-plane responsiveness.

Impact on Cluster Availability

Without etcd, or when etcd loses quorum the control plane is unable to respond to writes. New Pods are not possible to schedule and resources updates fail and stalls during the reconciliation process. Since etcd is at the foundation of all operations of a cluster, its health, latency, and recovery posture are platform reactions.

etcd is the key-value store of the distributed state in Kubernetes. Ensuring the stability of quorum, low-latency commits, and consistent replication is necessary to ensure that cluster is reliable, predictable and resilient in the event of failure.

4.4 Debugging transient and cascading failures

Modern Kubernetes environments operate as highly dynamic, distributed systems where failures are rarely isolated events. Contrary to monolithic architectures, a problem affecting the cloud-native platform can tend to disappear quickly and vanish before conventional monitoring can gather enough details. These temporary failures are referred to as transient failures and they make it difficult to diagnose the root cause as the symptoms can be gone but the side effects still occur in other areas of the system.

Cascading failures are an even more difficult challenge. A fault that is localized eg. a sluggish dependency, depleted resource, or network partition can spread across the services via retries, backpressure, and resource competition. Small disturbances in Kubernetes, where microservices constantly communicate and control plane components arrange the changes of states, may spread to instability of the entire system unless they are contained swiftly.

These patterns of failures cannot be debugged by inspecting logs or using alerting based on threshold. Engineers should have knowledge of inter-service dependencies, retry behavior, and time out configuration and the feedback mechanisms autoscaling and self-healing provide. Observability has to be spread over infrastructure, application layers and control plane operations to be able to reconstruct the timelines of failures accurately.

Strategies that work are aimed at isolating the blast radius, correlating distributed signals, and failure amplification mechanisms. Through aggregation of traces, metrics, logs, and event stream, teams are able to identify whether an anomaly is a fleeting anomaly, a sign of more systemic pressure, or the onset of a cascading degradation situation.

4.4.1 Identifying Transient Failure Patterns and Signal Volatility

Transient failures are temporary, periodic disruptions, which manifest themselves momentarily and vanish without leaving a long-term trace. Such failures are widespread and even challenging to replicate in distributed Kubernetes environments. A request can have a time out failure on the first attempt and then succeed on subsequent attempt. Before alerts, a pod can rejoin and relaunch again. A network connection is an aspect that will automatically restart itself after a few seconds after an automatic hanging. The rapid recovery of such failures has made them in most cases, obscure to traditional monitoring systems based on hard-coded thresholds or regular health returns. Nevertheless, despite being short lived, transient failures can lead to user experiences being poor, to retry storms, and to affected service crashes. Transient failures do not apply to cloud-native systems but is a usual experience with dynamically distributed environment. The ruse lies in the fact that the benign fluctuations and symptoms of systemic instability have to be separated.

Common Sources of Transient Failures in Kubernetes

Dynamic nature of distributed systems is usually associated with emergent transient problems:

- **Network latency spikes** due to congestion, packet loss, or short-lived routing instability
- **Ephemeral pod restarts** caused by OOM kills, image pull delays, or scheduling contention
- **Unavailability** Due to short-term dependency Problems like a database connection pool temporarily exceeding capacity.
- **Autoscaling delays**, where new pods are not yet ready to absorb increased traffic
- **Control plane latency**, especially during API server or etcd performance fluctuations

These occurrences can fix themselves, but recurrence suggests underlying systemic stress.

Recognizing Signal Volatility in Telemetry

Signal volatility is unpredictable fast changes in observability data. The system has oscillating trends like: instead of fixed measures.

- Sudden spikes in latency followed by rapid normalization
- Brief bursts of HTTP 5xx errors
- Temporary increases in pod restart counts
- Short-lived CPU or memory saturation events

Isolated volatility may be benign. But when the frequency or amplitude of these fluctuations increases, this is frequently a precursor of new cascading risk.

Why Transient Failures Are Hard to Detect

The traditional monitoring has problems with the ephemeral patterns due to:

- Static thresholds ignore short-duration anomalies
- Sampling intervals may miss micro-outages
- Alerting systems suppress short-lived spikes to reduce noise
- Logs may rotate before investigation begins

However, the failure has vanished by the time engineers get to investigate it.

It is therefore critical that observability is essential. High-resolution metrics, across service distribution tracing, and correlation can be used to rebuild transient events once they occur. **Detecting Patterns Instead of Events**

The most important one is that the primary attention should be paid not to individual failure but to behavioral trends:

- Track **error rate bursts over time**, not just sustained thresholds
- Analyze **retry amplification patterns** in client services
- Correlate **latency spikes across dependent services**
- Observe increasing **variance in performance metrics**, not just averages

With repeated transient failures, it is common to be early indicators of resource exhaustion, misconfigured timeouts, failure to implement adequate backoff strategies or dependency instability.

From Transient to Cascading Risk

While a single transient event may be harmless, clusters of transient failures can trigger cascading effects:

- Retries amplify load
- Latency spreads across service chains
- Circuit breakers trip
- Autoscalers overreact
- Control plane components experience elevated pressure

Early detection of these volatile situations helps to avoid the growth of these transient disturbances into large scale outages.

In the current Kubernetes setup, temporary failures are bound to happen. The aim is not to kill them all, but to study their trends, quantify their prevalence and how they propagate so that they become cascading failures.

4.4.2 Cascading Failure Propagation and Dependency Mapping

Small faults continue to be a constant problem in large computer systems. These mistakes can occasionally be swiftly fixed. In other cases, an error causes a related issue that either spreads to another area of the system or feeds back into the original problem. A cascading failure is the result of a rising number of failures brought on by positive feedback mechanisms.

Errors that result in feedback loops are far more dangerous than those that stand alone. Initially, a distributed system can see a slight decrease in capacity, an increase in mistakes, or a rise in delay. As additional components of the system attempt to compensate, they can unintentionally amplify the problem.

For example, if one server in a group experiences excess load and fails, the load may shift to neighboring servers. If those servers cannot handle the additional demand, they fail as well. The overload continues to propagate, snowballing into system-wide collapse.

Common Feedback Triggers

Cascading failures are often triggered by:

- Load spikes and overload
- An excessive number of client retries
- The depletion and limitations of resources
- Memory and CPU problems
- Starvation of threads

- Failover based on proximity
- Modifications to configurations and new rollouts
- Prolonged startup times or a changed traffic mix

Spikes in load are expected in real-world systems. They cannot be eliminated, but the way a system reacts to abnormal load determines whether it stabilizes or collapses.

Recovering From a Cascading Failure

It is frequently very difficult to recover from a cascading disaster. Under severe conditions, the system might need a manual control or complete shut down since it is not capable of automatically regaining its balance.

Dependency Mapping

Dependency mapping is the art of determining and drawing a diagram of the relationship among applications, services, infrastructure, and third-party components. It gives a living list of relationships within a system and assists groups to know the way failures spread.

Dependency mapping, rather than the previous use of outdated documentation, establishes actionable graphs that will provide answers to such questions like the following: What services will go down, in case this database becomes unavailable? What are the external APIs of this application?

"Application dependency mapping" (ADM) captures intended architecture as well as actual runtime behaviour. Design-time dependencies can be observed with the help of the static analysis and in the runtime telemetry, actual service-to-service interactions can be diagnosed. The combination of them offers a complete picture that makes the incident response speedy and the blast radius better understood during cascading failures.

4.4.3 Correlation, Containment, and System Recovery Strategies

Malfunctions of distributed Kubernetes systems are not normally run in a vacuum. On the face of it, an increase in latency may appear to be independent of either an increase in error rates or an instance of a pod restart. However, in order to engage in significant debugging, there is need to match signals across services, layers and time windows to reconstruct what actually happened.

Without any correlation, engineers would have no design but research symptoms. They could locate causal correlating chains.

Root Cause Analysis and Correlation.

Root cause analysis (RCA) focuses on the actual cause of a problem and not the surface effects of the problem. This is required in distributed systems which involves a process of matching several telemetry signals
Malfunctions of distributed Kubernetes systems are not normally run in a vacuum. On the face of it, an increase in latency may appear to be independent of either an increase in error rates or an instance of a pod restart. However, in order to engage in significant debugging, there is need to match signals across services, layers and time windows to reconstruct what actually happened.

Without any correlation, engineers would have no design but research symptoms. They could locate causal correlating chains.

Root Cause Analysis and Correlation.

Root cause analysis (RCA) focuses on the actual cause of a problem and not the surface effects of the problem. This is required in distributed systems which involves a process of matching several telemetry signals.

- Metrics that show latency, saturation, or error spikes
- Logs that capture exceptions or abnormal behavior
- Distributed traces that reveal request paths across services

Teams can get a failure traced back to the root by creating a chronology of events and connecting the various signals. As an example, the database connection exhaustion can be linked to a spike in API latency and be caused by the overloads in upstream services in the cases of a retry traffic. Correlation takes the individual alerts and converts them into consistent narratives on failed systems.

Containment Strategies and Blast Radius Control

Once a failure is detected, the next objective is containment—preventing the issue from spreading further.

Common containment patterns include:

- **Circuit breakers**, which stop repeated calls to an unhealthy service
- **Timeouts and bounded retries**, which prevent retry amplification
- **Bulkheads and resource isolation**, which separate workloads to avoid shared resource collapse
- **Rate limiting**, which protects downstream systems from overload

Containment limits the blast radius of a failure. Instead of allowing overload or instability to cascade through service dependencies, the system fails gracefully and locally.

System Recovery Mechanisms

Even with containment, recovery must be deliberate and structured. Resilient systems are designed with the assumption that failures will occur and must be recoverable.

Recovery strategies include:

- **Automatic restarts and self-healing controllers**
- **Failover to redundant replicas**
- **Checkpointing and rollback mechanisms**
- **Graceful degradation**, where non-critical functionality is temporarily disabled

Reconciliation loops in Kubernetes environments constantly compare the desired and actual state, and in conditions of stabilization of underlying conditions, automatic recovery is provided.

Good recovery minimizes downtime, predictability in restoration of service and minimizes the operational stress in cases of incident.

- Correlation is the determiner of the cause.
- Containment restricts the distribution.
- Stabilization of the situation is done by recovery.

A combination of these strategies converts cascading incidents due to catastrophic outages into manageable and observable incidents in distributed cloud-native systems.

4.5 Reducing Mean Time to Recovery (MTTR)

"Mean Time to Recovery" (MTTR) is one of the most important dependability metrics in modern cloud-native systems. It is a scale of rapidity with which a system can be restored to normalcy following the occurrence of a failure. Distributed Kubernetes systems inevitably experience failures - it is not the ability to fail at all, but the speed of recovery, that distinguishes a robust system with fragile one.

With the change of architectures into microservices and multi-cluster deployments, as well as hybrid infrastructures, the notion of incident response becomes significantly more complex. One problem facing a single user can include many services, layers of infrastructure, and control plane components. Without structured detection, correlation and response processes, there will be an exponential increase in the recovery time, which will increase the operational risk and impact on the user.

Simple fast troubleshooting cannot be successful in reducing MTTR. It must be highly observable, have automated remediation processes, clear on-escalation process, and strict after-incident learning. The diagnosis must be factual, the identification fast and recovery rate recurrent. The recovery mechanisms must take into account ephemeral workloads, autoscaling behaviour and control plane dependencies in highly dynamic environments like Kubernetes as well.

Lastly, MTTR depicts the maturity of an operation of a platform. Less downtime, improved customer experience, reduced financial impact, and high system resilience are directly transcripted to reduced MTTR. Recovery speed is not a post-design consideration and thus, this is one of the principles of a dependable cloud-native design.

4.5.1 Incident Detection and Early Signal Amplification

Identification of an unexpected intrusion or decline in the quality of a given IT service is known as incident detection. It applies system telemetry in order to identify the occurrence of performance variance at some extent relative to the anticipated baseline.

Detection Incident detection is the process of detecting an abnormality of the normal system behavior that suggests a possible service disruption or security threat. It is based on automated instruments to track telemetry information and issue warning signals when specific thresholds or patterns are violated.

Prior to formal incident detection, engineering teams used manual system failure detection. Outages were frequently reported by the users. This invisibility resulted in high “Mean Time to Repair (MTTR) since the problems were concealed until they resulted in complete failure of the service. Incident detection also provides automated mechanisms of detecting anomalies before they affect the end user.

Key Components of Incident Detection

- **Telemetry collection**: System is used to collect real time data like logs, metrics and traces of infrastructure and applications.
- **Token checking:** An alert is raised as soon as a particular metric such as CPU load or error rate surpasses a given threshold.
- **Anomaly detection**: Algorithms detect the abnormal patterns that are not in line with past baseline operation.
- **Alerting logic**: The system compares incoming data to rules in order to ascertain whether a notification is to be released.
- **Event correlation**: Monitoring tools compile related signals to differentiate between a local failure and a global outage.
- **Signal-to-noise ratio:** Effective detection concentrates on high-confidence notifications to avoid notification fatigue due to false positives.

Detecting of incidences is based on constant observation. The system measures performance metrics and logs, sets a normal behaviour baseline, comparisons real-time data to thresholds or past trends, detects anomalies, and sends out alerts when anomalies are established.

Golden Signals as Early Warning Indicators

In modern distributed systems, reliability can degrade gradually due to delayed reactions, deteriorating infrastructure, or increased error rates. Site Reliability Engineers can spot these warning indicators early with the use of golden signals in monitoring.

The majority of production events exhibit early warning indicators in one or more of the four Golden Signals—latency, traffic, mistakes, or saturation—prior to a complete outage, according to Google's Site Reliability Engineering teams. Teams can identify and address problems early, frequently before users are affected, by keeping an eye on these signals.

Every SRE tracks the following four Golden Signals:

- **Latency**: The time it takes a system to reply to a request is measured by latency. The first signal to deteriorate is frequently latency. Inefficient code routes, database contention, overloaded services, or problems with downstream dependencies can all be indicated by high latency. SREs track latency percentiles (p95 or p99) rather than averages since averages don't provide a full picture.
- **Traffic**: Traffic measures demand on the service, such as requests per second or transactions per minute. The examination of traffic patterns can help SREs understand how traffic is usually used, the maximum loads, and the unusual behaviour. Misstatements and delays mean rather different things in low-traffic times compared with times of peak demand.
- **Errors:** Errors track the number of failed requests, e.g. timeouts, HTTP 5xx responses, and failed API calls. This is because the SREs observe error ratios instead of actual counts to ensure reliability within a reasonable range of risk.
- **Saturation**: Saturation shows the proximity of the system to its limits. Its priorities are metrics such as queue depth, memory use, network bandwidth and CPU utilisation. Saturation gives warning to teams when the system hits its capacity upper limits and contributes to avoid cascading failures.

Signal Amplification and Correlation

The Golden Signals represent a practical approach to monitoring due to the various angles associated with each metric that covers health of the system:

- Latency is a concept that is concerned with user experience.
- Traffic explains load and demand patterns.
- Errors reveal reliability breakdowns.
- Saturation exposes capacity risks.

Alerts should not be taken separately. Latency notification must be observed hand in hand with the growing saturation or traffic. The objective of Golden Signals, which relies on correlation is broken in the case of processing of alerts in isolation.

In successful incident detection, there is a preference on actionable metrics. A measure is not supposed to create alarms when it does not spur action. Teams multiply meaningful early warnings and minimize noise by integrating threshold detection, anomaly detection and correlated Golden Signals.

When Golden Signals show a shift, it is time to investigate and take action before the degradation evolves into a full outage.

4.5.2 Automation, Runbooks, and Response Orchestration

A set of recorded operating procedures for carrying out particular IT tasks or procedures is called a "run book." Within an enterprise, runbooks offer a programmed way to install, start, stop, and support systems regularly. Runbooks facilitate efficiency and consistency, streamline new recruit onboarding, and enhance knowledge transfer between teams and people by standardising operations.

Runbooks are typically managed by IT Ops team members as part of an entire IT infrastructure library (ITIL) that also contains rules and best practices. Operations based on runbooks can be:

- Manual, requiring a human to follow detailed instructions.
- Semi-automated, meaning that automation programs like Chef or Ansible carry out some tasks while others are done by hand.
- Automated, requiring minimal human involvement to finish the procedure.

The majority of runbooks nowadays are at least partially automated. After all, runbook automation's documented, repeatable processes make it relatively simple to adopt. Because of this, it's perfect for businesses seeking rapid productivity gains without requiring a lot of setup or configuration. It's crucial to remember that runbook automation is mostly concerned with system deployment rather than system-to-system business process coordination.

Automation in Incident Response

Automation reduces Mean Time to Recovery by removing repetitive, manual tasks during incidents. On the triggering of alerts, the automated workflows may take the following predefined actions:

- Restarting failed services
- Scaling workloads
- Collecting diagnostic logs
- Rotating traffic away from unhealthy nodes
- Updating incident tickets

Automation lowers the cognitive load to the team as well as avoids the delays associated with manual involvement in recovery steps that can be predicted. Automation improves efficiency through uniformity of execution, reduces human error, and speedy remediation.

Response Orchestration

Response orchestration synchronises a variety of automated and manual responses on systems during an incident. Instead of handling alerts in isolation, orchestration connects monitoring tools, automation scripts, communication channels, and incident management platforms into a unified workflow.

When an alert meets defined conditions, orchestration systems can:

- Trigger automated remediation runbooks
- Notify the appropriate on-call engineers
- Create and update incident records
- Escalate severity based on impact
- Coordinate actions across dependent services

Response orchestration ensures that detection leads immediately to structured action. It prevents fragmented responses and aligns teams around a standardized recovery process.

- Automation executes tasks.
- Runbooks document procedures.
- Response orchestration connects systems and teams.

Together, they transform incident response from reactive troubleshooting into a coordinated, repeatable, and accelerated recovery process — directly reducing MTTR in distributed cloud-native environments.

4.5.3 Post-Incident Learning and Reliability Improvement Loops

An incident is not solved after the reliability process is completed. Every incident in the cloud native environment, in the mature form, will turn into a structured learning. It is not just a matter of re-establishing service, but also to learn how the failure spread, why, and what systemic flaws enabled it to reach that level.

Post incident learning converts outages to a long-term increase in reliability. In the absence of this feedback loop, teams will be prone to repeat the same tendencies under slightly different circumstances. A sustainable reduction of the MTTR should be in the form of transferring the experience of operation to the architectural, procedure, and monitoring improvements.

Blameless Postmortems

A postmortem is a written description of an incident, which records the occurrence of an incident, the effect, causative factors, and fundamental causes, and remediation. Successful post-mortems centre on systems and processes and not on the individual errors.

The fact that blameless post-mortems allow engineers to share freely without any fear of reprimand, makes the environment conducive to share knowledge. This promotes transparency and assists in revealing more root systemic issues such as:

- Insufficient monitoring coverage
- Misconfigured alert thresholds
- Weak retry or timeout strategies
- Hidden service dependencies
- Capacity planning gaps

A well-structured postmortem includes a clear timeline, technical analysis, and actionable follow-up items. Action items must be tracked to completion; otherwise, the learning loop breaks.

From Insights to System Improvements

The study of the event after the incident must directly impact the system design and functionality. Observability data, metrics, logs, and traces, are applied to not only fix the problem but also detect patterns and trends, which are signs of structural risks.

Common improvement areas include:

- Updating monitoring thresholds or adding new alerts
- Improving runbooks and automation workflows
- Adjusting resource limits or scaling policies
- Refactoring fragile service dependencies
- Enhancing redundancy or failover mechanisms

When incident insights lead to measurable improvements, reliability increases over time rather than stagnating.

Continuous Reliability Feedback Loops

Design Reliability engineering is a process. Every incident contributes to a loop of detection refinement, automation improvement, architectural hardening and process improvement.

Such a feedback loop is usually structured as follows:

1. Incident detection and mitigation
2. Root cause analysis
3. Documentation and postmortem
4. Corrective measures.
5. Improvement monitoring and validation.

This loop over time minimizes recurring failures, decreases future recovery time and enhances the overall system resilience.

- Post-incident education makes sure that the mitigation of MTTR does not last short term.
- It transforms engineering stress to operational stress.
- It alters proactive reliability evolution into reactive firefighting.

In distributed Kubernetes systems, reliability is not attained by avoiding all failures to occur - it is attained by learning about all failures and continually enhancing the system in response to a disruption in the future.

Multiple-Choice Questions (MCQs)

1. **Why is traditional monitoring often insufficient in distributed Kubernetes systems?**

   A) It consumes too little storage
   B) It focuses only on static infrastructure health
   C) It automatically fixes failures
   D) It removes the need for logging

2. **Which of the following best represents the three pillars of observability?**

   A) Security, storage, and backup
   B) Metrics, logs, and distributed tracing
   C) CPU, memory, and disk
   D) Scheduling, scaling, and deployment

3. **What is the primary purpose of metrics in Kubernetes observability?**

   A) To capture request flow across services
   B) To provide numerical measurements of system behavior
   C) To replace application logs
   D) To debug source code automatically

4. **Which observability signal is most useful for understanding the exact sequence of a request across multiple microservices?**

   A) Metrics
   B) Logs
   C) Distributed tracing
   D) Backups

5. **In Kubernetes, control plane observability mainly helps engineers monitor components such as:**

   A) Photoshop and Excel
   B) kube-apiserver, etcd, scheduler, and controller manager

C) Docker Hub and GitHub only
D) CDN and firewall rules only

6. A transient failure in Kubernetes is best described as:

A) A permanent hardware replacement
B) A short-lived issue that may disappear on retry
C) A planned software upgrade
D) A security audit event

7. What is a cascading failure in a distributed Kubernetes environment?

A) A failure that remains isolated to one pod forever
B) A failure that spreads from one component to multiple dependent services
C) A successful rollout of a new deployment
D) A backup operation running in sequence

8. Which of the following practices most directly helps reduce Mean Time to Recovery (MTTR)?

A) Ignoring alerts during peak hours
B) Faster incident detection, diagnosis, and automated remediation
C) Increasing the number of pods without analysis
D) Disabling logs to improve performance

9. Why are logs important in debugging Kubernetes systems?

A) They provide detailed event and error records for troubleshooting
B) They only measure CPU usage
C) They replace the need for tracing
D) They are used only for billing purposes

10. Which combination is most effective for diagnosing complex failures in Kubernetes?

A) Only CPU graphs
B) Only application screenshots

C) Metrics, logs, and traces used together
D) Restarting all nodes immediately

Answer

1	2	3	4	5	6	7	8	9	10
B	B	B	C	B	B	B	B	A	C

Chapter 5

Security, Identity, And Policy At Scale

5.1 Kubernetes Security Architecture

Kubernetes was also created to execute the coordination of containers at mass scale, but as clusters grow bigger and more complex, security turns into a fundamental feature rather than an output. Distributed cloud-native environments are dynamic, possess APIs, and control plane handle thousands of objects simultaneously. Absence of formal security architecture may also prove the very flexibility that Kubernetes provides to its advantage within a very brief amount of time.

This is because security in Kubernetes is not dependent on the layer. It passes through the container runtime, networking, worker nodes, and control plane. Each element provides the attack surface. The way to get the cluster security is to employ workload isolation, least privilege access, communication channels, and system state validation in a defence-in-depth approach.

Kubernetes environments are very dynamic unlike the traditional monolithic systems. Pods are short-lived, services are automatically scaled, and provisions are frequently changed. The security controls should be dynamic enough to keep up with this dynamism without reducing the speed of development. There is a secure Kubernetes architecture that balances security and agility of operations.

The knowledge of Kubernetes security architecture implies the knowledge of how the boundaries of trust are established, how components authenticate and authorize one another, and how the policies are established within the workloads. These mechanisms need to be predictable, monitorable and traceable at scale.

5.1.1 Control Plane and Node Security Boundaries

Throughout the cluster's whole lifespan, including the control plane, APIs, pods, and more, Kubernetes security offers protection. Strong defences against threat actors can be established by implementing defence-in-depth techniques to safeguard orchestration infrastructure and containers. Protect K8s containers from harmful behaviour and data leaks by implementing security policies, access control, encryption, and other measures.

Control Plane Security Boundary

The Kubernetes cluster's management component is the control plane. It consists of cloud-controller-manager, kube-controller-manager, kube-scheduler, etcd, and kube-apiserver. It is one of the most crucial resources in Kubernetes to secure since it connects the different components of a cluster.

For Kubernetes control plane security, use TLS. Use Transport Layer Security (TLS) to encrypt data while it's in transit and while it's at rest. Data delivered to and from control plane clients as well as data kept in the control plane fall under this category. Workload data that is at rest should be encrypted separately.

Make sure your company has policies and technologies in place to secure etcd. Organisations must restrict read and write access since etcd functions as a key-value store. Use etcd access control lists (ACL) and role-based access control (RBAC) to restrict account access to those who truly require it. Use strong credentials for access between etcd and the Kubernetes API and adhere to the principle of least privilege (POLP) to offer permissions to a small number of admin-level accounts. For a multi-layered defence strategy, think about isolating etcd behind firewalls and other network security measures.

Use RBAC to secure the Kubernetes API. Only queries that it can correctly authenticate and authorise will be answered by the Kubernetes API. The RBAC policies you set up control API authorisation and authentication; therefore the API is only as safe as your RBAC policies. Basic best practices for guaranteeing Kubernetes API security include developing safe RBAC policies that enforce POLP and provide permissions on a granular basis.

By utilising admission controllers, you may improve API security even more. An optional secondary layer of protection against requests that shouldn't be permitted is provided by admission controllers, which assess requests after the API server has already verified and approved them. By setting up secure certificates and mandating that the API server deliver requests on a secure port, network-level security for API queries can also be achieved.

Node Security Boundary

The servers that make up Kubernetes clusters are called nodes. Kubernetes nodes should be secured using the same security techniques as any other kind of server.

Kubernetes node security techniques consist of:

- To reduce your attack surface, remove unnecessary programs, libraries, and other operating system components.
- Install lightweight Linux distributions on nodes.
- Get rid of user accounts that aren't needed.
- Make sure that nothing executes as root unless absolutely required.

- Implement operating system hardening frameworks such as SELinux or AppArmor.
- To find potential breaches, gather and examine OS logs.

Making sure the master node is locked down is a crucial part of tightening node security. Although there are no essential distinctions between protecting a worker node and a master node, master node security is more crucial as a breach could harm your cluster more severely.

5.1.2 Securing Workloads and the Container Runtime

Security professionals and app development experts are aware that runtime security risks are real, even though we typically think of them as a collection of vulnerabilities and events that happen while programs are running. The actual software that tells containers how to operate and communicate with one other as well as the host system is called a container runtime.

As the execution layer that oversees the lifespan of containers from creation to termination and offers isolation, the capital "R" Runtime is essential to the container ecosystem. For many of the security issues that come up in containerised settings, it is therefore Ground Zero.

High-Level Container Runtime

- **Docker Engine:** Probably the most well-known high-level container runtime, Docker facilitates the development, deployment, and operation of apps and services in a containerised environment on any Linux or Windows platform. Scaling, load balancing, and monitoring of containerised applications are made possible by the Kubernetes API's ability to manage Docker containers within a Kubernetes architecture.
- **CRI-O:** Specifically created to work with Kubernetes, CRI-O is a high-level, lightweight container runtime. CRI-O is used in

Kubernetes settings to pull images from different registries, spin up containers, manage storage, and carry out user workloads in Kubernetes pods. It is completely compliant with the CRI (Container Runtime Interface).

- **Podman:** An open source, Linux-native utility that specialises in operating containers without a daemon, Podman is an alternative to Docker. Podman uses an OCI-compliant runtime, such as runc or crun, to communicate with the operating system and generate the running containers, just like the majority of other popular engines.

Low-Level Container Runtime

- **containerd:** containerd manages the whole container lifecycle of its host system, including network attachments, low-level storage, image transmission and storage, and container execution and supervision. It operates under the kubelet in a Kubernetes environment, which interacts with containerd to execute containers in accordance with Pod specifications.
- **runc:** This is the default runtime that supports higher-level runtimes such as CRI-O and Docker. It focuses on using OCI requirements for container spawning and operation.
- The OCI runtime standard is implemented by the low-level C runtime crun, which is optimised for speedy container execution and minimum overhead in terms of performance and resource efficiency.
- **runhcs:** Mainly focused on Windows containers, runhcs bridges the gap between Kubernetes orchestration and running containers on the Windows OS by allowing nodes to manage and run Windows-based containers.

Container Runtime Security Issues

- **Software supply chain:** An essential part of a containerised architecture are images. These static files with executable code are used to pre-configure and pre-populate containers. Container images are, in theory, unchangeable. In reality, malware and vulnerabilities might exist in container images. Malware, backdoors, and other unpatched security flaws can occasionally be found in images from unreliable sources.

- **Inadequate Isolation Between Containers:** Inadequate isolation exposes the environment to a concerning potential as containers and their host share the same operating system kernel: An attacker may be able to compromise other containers in the environment or even the host system itself if one container is compromised.
- **Privilege Escalation:** To obtain elevated privileges, attackers often take use of container flaws. Elements of the containerised environment frequently have higher-level access than they really require for regular operation due to misconfigurations or the usage of default privileges. Another common cause of runtime compromise is the leakage of container secrets, such as database credentials or API keys.
- **Kubernetes security:** By default, containers frequently have parameters that put usability ahead of security. Configuration drift, which occurs when systems or human insertion make poorly-advised changes, exacerbates this problem even further. The entire container's cash is at risk during runtime after certain parameters, including file permissions and network settings, have strayed too far from the secure baseline.

Container Runtime Security Best Practices

- **Regular Container Image Updates:** Apply the most recent security updates to container images on a regular basis. Use tracking programs that look for vulnerabilities and configuration changes in the pictures and send out notifications when potential configuration drift is found.
- **Effective Isolation Techniques:** Use isolation techniques like SELinux and AppArmor, as well as container-specific kernel features like namespaces and cgroups, to limit access to kernel features and offer stricter separation across containers.

- **Principles of Least Privilege:** Use as few rights as possible while running containers. Restrict kernel capabilities whenever possible, and limit root-level access to what is absolutely necessary.
- **Lock Down Orchestration Platforms:** Security should be the primary consideration when configuring platforms such as Kubernetes. Use Role-Based Access Control (RBAC) and network policies to secure cluster interactions.
- **Frequent Security Audits:** Make sure that Kubernetes audit logging is enabled and conduct regular security audits and reviews to find misconfigurations or departures from security best practices.

5.1.3 Network Security and Segmentation

One particularly complicated aspect of Kubernetes is networking. There are numerous ways to configure networks. While some of the resources in your cluster need direct connection to the Internet, others might simply interface with internal networks. The dynamic configuration of ports, IP addresses, and other network characteristics can make it challenging to monitor network activity.

Kubernetes network security can be particularly difficult due to these intricacies. It necessitates a thorough comprehension of the networking architecture of Kubernetes as well as knowledge with the native network security tools that Kubernetes provides, including network policies and third-party solutions that can further harden networks.

Kubernetes Networking Fundamentals

Networks have two primary functions in Kubernetes:

- **Internal networks:** Networks manage internal traffic that enables pods, Kubernetes nodes, and other cluster resources to communicate with one another. Internal networks are usually segregated from the public Internet and employ private subnets and IP addresses.

- **External networks:** Public IP addresses are used by workloads that must connect to the Internet.

The service that controls traffic flows inside Kubernetes is called kube-proxy. Each node in a Kubernetes cluster runs kube-proxy, which redirects traffic to containers hosted on those nodes according to the IP addresses and ports of the containers.

To construct a virtual network interface that containers can use, Kubernetes often employs a Container Network Interface (CNI) plugin. Kubernetes may be integrated with a number of third-party network configuration management systems using CNI plugins. The majority of production clusters utilise CNIs to control networking, even though it is technically possible to configure networking in Kubernetes without a CNI plugin.

To make networking easier, production Kubernetes clusters usually make use of a service mesh. The discovery of various resources on a network is automated by service meshes. Additionally, the majority of service meshes offer security and network observability features. Although it can integrate with popular service meshes, Kubernetes does not have a native service mesh.

Dynamic Configurations and Security Challenges

As those resources are established, IP addresses and ports for nodes, pods, and services are immediately setup. Static IP addresses cannot usually be assigned using native tooling, even though administrators can specify pools of IP addresses that Kubernetes will use to perform assignments.

Kubernetes network security is made more challenging by dynamic configurations. Unlike virtual machines, hosts cannot be whitelisted or blacklisted based on static address configurations. Additionally, a given IP address may be reassigned when a resource shuts down, making it more challenging to match network traffic data to specific services within Kubernetes.

Define Network Policies

Network policies are the most significant native resource that Kubernetes provides for network security. Network policies specify guidelines that control network-level communication between pods.

Network policies give administrators the ability to specify networking rules according to context, including namespaces and pod labels. This is important since Kubernetes networking settings are dynamic, making IP addresses unreliable for managing network rules.

Kubernetes RBAC policies and network policies are comparable. These are files that indicate which networking rules are applicable and which resources—like a namespace or a pod—are covered by the rules.

5.1.4 Secrets Management and Data Protection

Within a Kubernetes cluster, secrets safely store private data including SSH keys, OAuth tokens, and passwords. In order to maintain confidentiality and prevent unwanted access, Kubernetes offers an object called Secret that allows you to handle secrets independently of the application code.

Applications can be deployed securely within a Kubernetes cluster thanks to the Kubernetes Secrets system. Without keeping the sensitive data inside the application, the authorized pods have access to secrets and can retrieve them when needed. Additionally, Kubernetes provides tools for these secrets to be updated continuously, increasing the security and integrity of private data.

Best Practices for Managing Secrets in Kubernetes

1. **Implementing RBAC Policies**

Role-based access control (RBAC) simplifies permission management in Kubernetes, which defines who is authorized to access secrets and what operations they are allowed to perform. RBAC implements the minimal privilege principles by clearly assigning roles and permissions to ensure that there is no unauthorized access to secret data in Kubernetes settings. This model facilitates a fine-grained access control.

The RBAC policies of Kubernetes are also dynamic and the companies can customize the amount of control in various teams and workloads. These roles are configured by administrators, who apply an exact set of rules to match operational access controls to an existing set of predefined security requirements. The introduction of the RBAC policies as the key practice contributes to the protection of sensitive information within Kubernetes clusters.

2. Regularly Rotating Secrets

Turning secrets regularly is vital in ensuring that there is a secure Kubernetes environment, and secret credentials are not exposed over an extended time. Rotation refers to the periodic refresh of secret data, which other data minimizes the harm that this data can cause in case of leakage. The given practice assists proactive security management by minimizing window vulnerabilities.

Secret rotation is automated in Kubernetes by default, and the changes can be reflected without disrupting the running services. The incorporation of rotation into CI/CD pipelines allows the consistent updates during the stages of deployment. One of the preventive mechanisms contributing to better data security and reducing the threats of unauthorized access in Kubernetes apps is regular secret rotation.

3. Avoiding Hardcoding Secrets

Hardcoding secrets is also very risky as it exposes sensitive information to the application code, which becomes available in the source control system and on-demand. To reduce this risk, the developer must externalize secrets, which is achieved by using Kubernetes Secrets to save them so that they are not exposed. This practice isolates configuration information and code.

With environment variables and volumes mapped by Kubernetes, secrets are not visible to applications, and they are accessed through secure means. Access controls also help to guard secrets and reduce the risk of accidental disclosure or unauthorized access. The hardcoded secrets are important to avoid in protection of sensitive information.

4. Auditing and Monitoring Access

Access to Kubernetes Secrets is to be audited and monitored to ensure that the usage of the Secrets is not misused and that unauthorized activities are not carried out. Application of logging mechanisms enables one to see who accessed secrets and when these occurred. It helps to identify anomalies or breaches, allowing a quick resolution of possible security incidents in the Kubernetes world with the help of this ability.

Secret access patterns can be measured using monitoring tools that are built into Kubernetes and compare data with the expected behaviors. These insights are utilized by the administrators in order to tighten their security policies and guarantee that only authorized individuals handle sensitive information. Maintaining properly documented audit trails and performing ongoing surveillance are two of the core practices in increasing the secrecy management effectiveness.

5. Using External Secret Management Tools

External secret management tools are used to provide Kubernetes with improved security and compliance functions, in addition to the native features. Integrations with systems such as HashiCorp Vault, Azure Key Vault, or AWS Secrets Manager offer a centralized management, advanced encryption policies, and full audit histories. They facilitate compliance requirements of high standards as well.

Using the external tools, the organizations can decouple secret management and Kubernetes, providing administrators with an interface to enforce policies and monitor access. These tools simplify the process of lifecycle management and allow secure rotations and imposing policies of decryption in various settings. The use of third-party secret management systems raises the security posture of Kubernetes.

6. Implementing Immutable Secrets

Immutable secrets are a type of security practice, in which once secret data is created, it cannot be changed. The principle makes sure that secrets retain their initial integrity in the course of time, which would reduce the risks of the accidental alterations or the unauthorized changes. The unchangeable secrets are especially useful in high compliance environments where data should be controlled strictly.

The immutable nature of secrets needs to be planned at the deployment phase and the applications must be configured to process immutable data without being disrupted. Kubernetes can apply such practices through limiting the modification of secrets using controlled mechanisms or specifying annotations that do not allow updates. Immutability model improves the integrity of data in Kubernetes.

7. Automating Secret Updates with Operators

The operators are Kubernetes extensions that are applied to the applications that provide an automatic update of their secrets. Operators simplify secret updates by encapsulating application-specific logic, which guarantees a consistent presentation of data across all activities involved in the management of deployments. Secret management systems decrease human supervision and decrease the number of mistakes, as well as ensure that the secret is updated regularly.

Operators-based secret management can help conciliate secret lifecycle approaches and agile practices, providing timely updates and keeping up with the latest security standards. This framework is conducive to dynamism, and fast deployments require frequent secret turnsover. The use of operators also highlights the versatility of Kubernetes, enhancing the efficiency of operations by maintaining security of sensitive information.

5.2 Identity and Access Management

Distributed Kubernetes environments make identity the basis of security. All incoming interactions within a cluster, regardless of whether they are generated by a human operator, by an automated system, or by an operational workload, are authenticated and authorized and are permitted to take actions. A well-configured cluster can be ruined by the too many permissions or erroneous credentials unless it has a solid "identity and access management" (IAM) frameworks.

Kubernetes is a very dynamic environment whereby pods are volatile, services are auto-scaled, and APIs are constantly invoked. Conventional perimeter-based security models cannot be utilized in such settings. Rather, security needs to be identity-based. No longer is the question where the request is coming, but becoming who is making the request, and what they may do.

Kubernetes does not limit its identity to human identity. There are identities of service accounts, controllers, nodes, and external systems that are all secured. All identities have to be authenticated, mapped to a specific role and limited based on the principle of least privilege. On a large scale, this necessitates a uniform policy implementation and top-down governance.

Identity and access management are effective to make it granular, auditable, and revocable. It minimizes the blast radius of compromised credential, it prevents privilege escalation and it sets a definite trust model over the cluster. IAM is not only a security operation but a platform governance in large organizations that have several clusters of operation.

5.2.1 Authentication Mechanisms in Kubernetes

When a user or service submits a request to the Kubernetes API server, authentication confirms their identity. It provides an answer to the query,

"Who are you?"

There isn't an integrated user management mechanism in Kubernetes. Rather, it depends on techniques of external authentication. The fundamental objective of all Kubernetes authentication methods is to verify the identity of the user or service submitting the authentication request in order to decide whether or not access should be allowed. A user's actions must be approved upon authentication, usually through a role-based access granting procedure.

Authentication Methods

- **Client Certificates (X.509):** Using an X.509 certificate to confirm the identity of the user submitting a request is one of Kubernetes' most straightforward authentication techniques. The main disadvantage of X.509 authentication is that it necessitates human certificate management, despite the fact that it is simple to set up. You must regenerate certificates when they expire to avoid interfering with authentication. Additionally, you must keep in mind to revoke certificates for people whose access you wish to restrict. It won't function well in production settings, but it might be suitable for small-scale clusters.
- **Bearer Tokens:** Static tokens stored in Kubernetes and used to authenticate requests to the API server.
- **Service Account Authentication Token:** To verify authentication requests, signed bearer tokens are used in service account token authentication. Make a service account before using this method. You can use this command to create a Kubernetes secret file that contains a bearer token for authentication. Implementing this strategy is not too difficult. However, in order to maintain access, the tokens must be renewed because they have a limited lifespan (usually twenty-four hours or less).
- **OIDC (OpenID Connect):** A method that integrates with identity providers like AWS IAM, Google, or Okta. You can establish your own or use one of the numerous public OIDC providers. The

main benefit of OIDC as a Kubernetes authentication technique is that, once set up, it will function continuously. However, based on the OIDC provider you choose, the implementation process varies and it is somewhat complicated to set up.

- **Webhook Token Authentication:** Users use tokens generated by an external service to authenticate over the Kubernetes API server. If you have authentication services that you use for other workloads and wish to apply the same procedure for Kubernetes authentication, this method may be practical.
- **Authentication Proxy:** Request value headers set by an authenticating proxy can be used by the Kubernetes API server to identify users. To ascertain whether a request is legitimate, authentication data, including usernames and namespaces, can be extracted from these headers. If you wish to authenticate using information saved in an external service, this way is helpful.

Example: Authenticating with OIDC

Let's say a developer wants to access an EKS cluster integrated with AWS IAM and OIDC. The authentication flow is:

- The developer runs a kubectl get pods command.
- Kubernetes verifies the identity using an OIDC token issued by AWS.
- If the token is valid, Kubernetes moves to the authorization step.
- If the token is invalid, Kubernetes rejects the request immediately.

5.2.2 Role-Based Access Control (RBAC) and Least Privilege

A security feature in Kubernetes called "role-based access control" (RBAC) can distinguish between a strong, safe cluster and one that is susceptible to internal threats and configuration errors. Fundamentally, RBAC establishes who is allowed to do what, where, and when in a

Kubernetes cluster. But RBAC is more than just authentication.

RBAC serves as a kind of main gatekeeper to everything that takes place within a Kubernetes cluster such that users and services may only gain access to what they require and nothing beyond that. It offers fine-grained authorization policies, which control the actions users, groups or service accounts may take on which resources. This granularity is needed in the multi-tenant clusters or environments with stringent compliance needs.

As an example, suppose that your development team requires access to deploy applications but they should be unable to access sensitive data in production namespaces. Or maybe you are incorporating a 3 rd party monitoring tool that needs read only access throughout the cluster. Unless you set up RBAC properly, you may end up giving too liberal permissions, which goes against the principle of least privilege and potentially leaves your cluster vulnerable to needless risks.

☛ Core RBAC Components

Permission is set by roles and Cluster Roles. These roles are bound to subjects, such as users, groups, or service accounts, by Role Bindings and Cluster Role Bindings.

Assign roles and Cluster Roles in order to indicate what can be done to the resources. Use Role Bindings and Cluster Role Bindings to assign these permissions to specific subjects.

☛ How RBAC Works in Kubernetes

Kubernetes RBAC is a system that establishes permissions in terms of roles, bindings and subjects. These elements collaborate with the intention of managing Kubernetes resources.

Request validation in Kubernetes API server is carried out through authentication (who you are) and authorization (what you can do). When a request hits the API server, it first authenticates the user through configured authentication plugins (like client certificates, bearer tokens, or OpenID Connect) and then checks RBAC rules to determine if the authenticated user has sufficient permissions.

5.2.3 Service Accounts and Workload Identity

One kind of non-human account that gives a Kubernetes cluster a unique identification is called a service account. The credentials of a particular Service Account can be used by Application Pods, system components, and entities both inside and outside the cluster to identify as that Service Account. This identity can be used for a number of purposes, such as setting identity-based security policies or authenticating to the API server.

In the API server, service accounts are represented as Service Account objects. Every Kubernetes namespace has a default Service Account when it is created, and every service account is associated with a certain namespace. You may easily build service accounts to enable particular tasks because they are lightweight and described in the Kubernetes API.

User accounts, which are verified human users in the cluster, are not the same as service accounts. The Kubernetes API server treats user IDs as opaque data by default and does not have user accounts.

Use Cases for Kubernetes Service Accounts

In the following situations, service accounts can be used to supply identities:

- The Kubernetes API server must be communicated with by pods.
- Pods must connect to an outside service.
- Using an image Pull Secret to authenticate to a private image registry.
- The Kubernetes API server must be communicated with via an external service.
- Third-party security software relies on the Service Account identity of different Pods to group those Pods into different contexts.

Using a service account for Kubernetes:

- Create a Service Account piece.
- Use an authorisation mechanism like RBAC to give the Service Account object permissions.
- When creating a pod, assign the Service Account object to it.

Workload Identity

Applications or services operating within a Kubernetes cluster are uniquely authenticated and authorised by a set of credentials or identifiers known as a workload identity. Access control and secure communication between various cluster components are made possible by workload identification.

Because Kubernetes environments are transient and dynamic, IP-based access controls are not feasible. In order to apply fine-grained security standards and guarantee that only authorised services can communicate with one another, workload IDs offer a way to confirm the identity of each workload.

In Kubernetes, workload identity enables pods to take on an identity, like an IAM role, which gives them particular rights to communicate with cloud services. Workload identity guarantees that each microservice is given only the necessary rights by giving each one a distinct identity, upholding the least privilege principle.

This method eliminates the need to store and manage long-lived service account keys while supporting short-lived and often rotating identities.

5.3 Policy enforcement mechanisms

Authentication and authorization are not the only thing that security can do in a present-day Kubernetes environment. Although identities have been verified and permission is granted appropriately, clusters need to have mechanisms to enforce operational, security, and compliance rules in a consistent manner. This is the extra control that is offered by policy enforcement mechanisms.

Kubernetes is both very dynamic and declarative. The automated pipelines, GitOps workflows and CI/CD systems ensure that resources are created, updated and deleted on a continuous basis. The lack of centralized policy enforcement allows misconfigs, insecure deployment, and the use of privileges to get into the cluster easily. The policy controls are applied to make sure that any request is accepted by meeting the predefined standards of security and governance.

Kubernetes is enforced on several levels. There are some controls that authenticate configuration at the API level, prior to the creation of resources. Other performance monitors constantly keep watch of the cluster state and workloads stay under control in the long run. Combined, these mechanisms assist organizations with the implementation of guardrails that keep them out of risky configurations, but allow developer agility.

Policy mechanisms lower attack surface by enforcing security baselines, compliance requirements and operational constraints, limit configuration drift and enable zero-trust architecture in Kubernetes clusters.

5.3.4 Admission Controllers and API-Level Policy Validation

Backend clusters in production are now much faster and easier to manage thanks to Kubernetes. Because of its adaptability, scalability, and user-friendliness, Kubernetes has become the de facto standard in container orchestration. Additionally, Kubernetes offers a number of capabilities that protect production workloads. A collection of plugins known as admission controllers is one such security feature. To utilize some of Kubernetes' more sophisticated security features, admission controllers must be enabled.

Admission Controllers

Kubernetes admission controllers are essentially plugins that regulate and enforce cluster usage. They act as gatekeepers, intercepting authenticated API requests and changing the request object or rejecting them completely.

The two stages of the admission control process are the validating phase and the mutating phase. Admission controllers can therefore function as either validating or modifying controllers, or as a combination of the two. For instance, the Limit Ranger admission controller can confirm that pods with explicitly defined resource requirements do not surpass the per-namespace restrictions indicated in the Limit Range object (validating phase) and supplement pods with default resource demands and limits (mutating phase).

It is important to note that admission controllers really regulate some parts of Kubernetes' operation that many users would consider built-in. For instance, the Namespace Lifecycle admittance controller stops any new objects from being created in a namespace that has been erased and is now in the Terminating state.

Two of the admission controllers that come with Kubernetes play a unique function due to their adaptability: Validating Admission Webhooks and Mutating Admission Webhooks. No policy decision logic is implemented by these admission controllers. Rather, the relevant activity is retrieved from a webhook, or REST endpoint, of a cluster-based service. By separating the admission controller logic from the Kubernetes API server, this method enables users to design custom logic that will run each time a resource is added, modified, or removed from a Kubernetes cluster.

Mutating admission webhooks have the ability to change objects, whilst validating admission webhooks do not. This is the distinction between the two types of admission controller webhooks. Nevertheless, requests might be rejected even by a changing admission webhook. The request object that a validating webhook sees is the final version that would be saved to etcd because validating admission webhooks are executed after mutating ones.

The Kubernetes API server receives a flag that configures the collection of enabled admission controllers. The --enable-admission-plugins flag took the role of the deprecated --admission-control flag.

5.3.5 Open Policy Agent (OPA) and Policy as code

A general-purpose, open-source policy engine called the Open Policy Agent (OPA, pronounced "oh-pa") unifies policy enforcement throughout the stack. OPA offers a high-level declarative language that allows you to declare policies as code and straightforward APIs that relieve your software of making policy decisions. OPA can be used to enforce rules in Kubernetes, microservices, API gateways, CI/CD pipelines, and more. OPA is a graduated Cloud Native Computing Foundation (CNCF) project.

OPA separates the formulation of policies from their implementation. Your software queries OPA and provides structured data (like JSON) as input when it needs to make policy judgements. Any structured data can be entered into OPA.

By comparing the query input to policies and data, OPA creates policy decisions. You can describe nearly any type of invariant in your policies because OPA and Rego are domain-agnostic. For instance:

- Which resources are accessible to which users?
- Which subnets are permitted to send out traffic?
- Which clusters a task needs to be assigned to.
- From which registries binaries are available for download.
- What OS features a container is capable of using.
- When it is possible to access the system.

Simple yes/no or allow/deny responses are not the only options for making policy decisions. Your policies can produce any kind of structured data as an output, just like query inputs.

Policy as Code

Instead of using documentation, policy as code establishes compliance standards in executable code. When changes take place, such as during the execution of the CI/CD pipeline, when Kubernetes is admitted, or when infrastructure configurations are applied, these rules automatically evaluate.

The basic change is from "trust and verify" to "verify then trust." Because they reveal windows of risk in days, traditional security methods employ first and audit later models. This is reversed by policy code, which verifies compliance before deployment and ensures that only authorised configurations reach production.

Two problems are separated by the compliance at the point of change (CAPOC) pattern:

- Compliance employees are assigned development tasks; they create SBOMs, do security scans, and test regulations locally.
- Admission controllers verify that the required checks were completed and passed at the deployment level.

Security teams maintain their enforcement power while developers are free to optimise their pipelines thanks to this separation.

How Policy Enforcement Works Technically

The code written in the form of policies is executed by admission controllers - elements that intercept requests in advance of the generation or alteration of resources. These controllers in Kubernetes environments compare all deployment, service, or configuration changes with specified policies.

The technical workflow:

- The developer submits a deployment (via an API, GitOps, or kubectl).
- The request is intercepted by the admission controller.
- The request is compared to current policies by the policy engine (OPA, Kyverno).
- The resource is either accepted by the controller or rejected with a thorough error message.

Rules are defined using declarative languages (Rego) in policy engines such as Open Policy Agent. A policy could confirm that resource limitations are included in all deployments, that cryptographic signatures demonstrate the provenance of artefacts, or that container images originate from reliable registries.

The fundamental architectural tenet is that policies are not hardcoded rules but rather templates. Reusable policy templates are defined and then instantiated with restrictions appropriate to the context.

5.3.6 Pod Security Standards and Workload Restrictions

Policies and principles for preserving container security and integrity in Kubernetes clusters are known as Kubernetes Pod Security Standards. In order to guarantee that containerized workloads are safe against known privilege escalations and follow the most recent Pod hardening best practices, the standards describe three distinct profiles with differing restrictions:

- **Privileged:** Offers a completely unconstrained policy.
- **Baseline:** Prevents known privilege escalations while providing minimally restrictive safeguards.
- **Restricted:** May restrict compatibility but adheres to current Pod hardening best practices.

Following these guidelines makes it easier to guarantee that containerized apps in Kubernetes settings satisfy industry-standard security requirements. To compare the isolation levels of Pods with these Pod Security Standards, Kubernetes provides an integrated Pod Security admission controller.

This was the responsibility of PodSecurityPolicy in earlier iterations of Kubernetes. But in version 1.21, Kubernetes deprecated this feature, and in version 1.25, it was completely deleted. It was difficult to determine which rights applied in a given scenario, and PodSecurityPolicy was prone to unintentionally providing permissions that were more expansive than intended. Pod Security Standards and the default Pod Security admission controller took its place once it was abandoned.

Operating Pod Security Admission Controller.

The admission control mode can be enabled in the namespaces when the Pod Security admission controller is enabled:

- Enforce: Rejects Violation of policy Pods.
- Audit: The violation of policy is permitted and an annotation of an audit is added to the record of the audit log event.
- Warn: Authorizes Pods having policy violation but warns users.

Configuration entails the identification of two labels:

- **Privilege:** Privileged, base, or restricted.
- **Mode:** Enforce, audit, or warn.

The Pod Security admission controller imposes such standards on clusters or namespaces, keeping the workloads within secure limits and also prevents possible privilege escalation and other malicious actions.

5.3.7 Runtime Policy Enforcement and Continuous Compliance

Kubernetes security policies are policies that regulate interactions and behaviours in your environment. These policies cover different areas of security like access control, network segmentation and workload restrictions and they can be used to comply and to secure your clusters. Security measures such as Network Policies and Admission Control Policies will also contribute to security by restricting unwarranted access, stipulating privileged container constraints, and controlled and secure workload setups.

The goal of Kubernetes runtime security is to protect containerised apps and the underlying Kubernetes infrastructure when they are in use. Runtime security monitors system calls, network traffic, and container activity to spot abnormalities or threats in real time. Throughout container operation, it guarantees that infrastructure and applications are protected from hackers and security breaches.

Runtime security is executed in situations where the security of the application is of interest in the containerized application during the runtime stage, by detecting and preventing unwanted access, privilege escalation attacks, and additional security threats. A successful runtime security policy encompasses the use of runtime security measures in the forms of runtime environment monitoring, implementation of security policies, and exploitation of runtime protection measures to mitigate the possible threats.

Kubernetes Runtime Security Tools.

- **Vulnerability detection and scanning: kube-bench and Kubescape.**

kube-bench is used to test the security of Kubernetes clusters against the standards created by the Center of Internet Security (CIS). It assesses Kubernetes configurations in order to verify that they are best practices related to component security and minimizing attack surface.

Kubescape is an evaluation of the security state of Kubernetes clusters. It identifies vulnerabilities, misconfigurations, and deviations as well as best-practice which offer an insight into the possible security risks.

- **Enforcement and management of policy: Open Policy Agent (OPA).**

The Open Policy Agent (OPA) is an open-source declarative policy-writing language designed to be used in expressing and applying policy across a Kubernetes ecosystem. It is built into Kubernetes, offering a single set of tools to manage security policies, admission control and configuration validation.

- **Real-time threat detection: Falco.**

Falco is specialized in real-time threat monitoring in Kubernetes. It tracks runtime activities of containers on a kernel level, identifying extraordinary activity and possible attacker threats in real time.

- **Continuous Compliance**

The use of Kubernetes generates a very dynamic ecosystem, which poses security and compliance challenges. In the situation the software is being run in Kubernetes clusters, it is required to gain complete observability of the containerized space, audit trail, and pay close attention to the networks and data flows to prevent unauthorized access.

The "Center of Internet Security" (CIS) Kubernetes Benchmark delivers industry-conformable guidelines on how to set up cluster elements to promote the safety stance of Kubernetes deployments. It contains Level 1 recommendations that are quite easy to implement and Level 2 defence-in-depth recommendations to mission-critical setups.

The National Institute of Standards and Technology (NIST) Application Container Security Guide identifies security issues related to the use of containerized applications and offers viable solutions to these issues.

The NSA and CISA Kubernetes hardening guidance describes specific threats to Kubernetes clusters and provides mitigation guidance in areas including pod security, network isolation, authentication and authorization, log auditing, and application security.

Continuous compliance requires leveraging built-in Kubernetes features such as log auditing, RBAC, and Admission Controllers, along with automated tools for vulnerability detection, log analysis, and security validation. A zero-trust model allows only authorized traffic and processes to be active in the environment, supporting continuous compliance and runtime policy enforcement.

5.4 Multi-tenancy and isolation

Included in most cloud-native environments are the workloads of various teams, business departments, or external customers that are hosted in the same Kubernetes cluster. This common use model is referred to as multi-tenancy. Multi-tenancy allows utilizing the resources more effectively, be cost-effective, and easy to operate, yet it also creates serious security and isolation issues.

Multi-tenancy in Kubernetes allows only tight logical and operational isolation between tenants so that they are not allowed to interfere with the workloads of another tenant, gain access to data that they do not have permission to access, or otherwise consume the available resources in an untenable manner. Failure to isolate a single compromised workload can cause security violation or failure domino effect to other tenants because of inadequate isolation mechanisms.

Kubernetes isolation is available on a variety of levels, such as namespaces, resource limits, role-based access control, and network segmentation, and node-level separation. All these mechanisms are used to assure that even workloads that are based on the same underlying cluster infrastructure are logically separated.

An effective multi-tenant architecture is one that balances the security and efficiency. It should implement stringent access control, privilege escalation, network isolation communication, and limit resource usage and at the same time allow teams to act independently even in a shared cluster environment.

5.4.1 Namespace-Based Architectural Boundaries and Resource Segmentation

A Namespace in Kubernetes offers a way to isolate collections of API resources inside a single cluster. There are two main aspects to this isolation:

1. Just like files in folders, object names within a namespace may overlap with names in other namespaces. Tenants can now list their resources without worrying about what other tenants are doing.
2. Namespaces are the scope of many Kubernetes security policies. Namespace-scoped resources include, for instance, Network Policies and RBAC Roles. Users and Service Accounts can be confined to a namespace using RBAC.

A Namespace aids in dividing a tenant's workload into a logical and discrete management unit in a multi-tenant setting. Even when a single tenant operates several workloads, it is actually standard practice to isolate each job in its own namespace. This guarantees that every task has a unique identification and can be set up with a suitable security policy.

To effectively isolate tenant workloads, the namespace isolation paradigm necessitates configuring a number of additional Kubernetes resources, networking plugins, and adherence to security best practices. These factors are covered in the section that follows.

Access controls

Authorisation is the most crucial kind of isolation for the control plane. Teams or their workloads can alter or disable all other kinds of policies, eliminating any protection those policies would provide, if they are able to access or edit each other's API resources. Because of this, it's crucial to make sure that each tenant has access to just the namespaces they require. The "Principle of Least Privilege" refers to this."

In the Kubernetes control plane, authorisation is frequently enforced for both users and workloads (service accounts) via role-based access control (RBAC). Functions and RolesAlthough they are less helpful for multi-tenant clusters, bindings are Kubernetes objects that are used at the namespace level to enforce access control in your application. Similar objects exist for granting access to cluster-level resources.

RBAC must be utilised in a multi-team setting to limit tenants' access to the proper namespaces and guarantee that only privileged users, like cluster administrators, can access or modify cluster-wide resources.

The namespace containing the impacted resources should probably be refactored into finer-grained namespaces if a policy ends up giving a user greater access than they require. By applying common RBAC policies to various namespaces while permitting fine-grained policies when needed, namespace management tools may make the administration of these finer-grained namespaces easier.

Quotas

Node resources like CPU and memory are consumed by Kubernetes workloads. Resource quotas can be used in a multi-tenant setting to control how tenant workloads consume resources. Resource quotas can be used to restrict the quantity of API resources (such as Pods or ConfigMaps) that a tenant may produce in the many teams use case, where tenants have access to the Kubernetes API. Limits on the number of objects provide equity and try to prevent other tenants who share a control plane from being impacted by noisy neighbours.

Quotas for resources are namespaced objects. Cluster administrators can employ quotas to prevent a tenant from monopolising a cluster's resources or overloading its control plane by mapping tenants to namespaces. Quota administration is made easier by namespace management solutions.

Additionally, certain namespace management systems allow groups of namespaces to share quotas, which gives administrators significantly more freedom with less work than built-in quotas, whereas Kubernetes quotas only apply within a single namespace.

By preventing a single tenant from using more resources than their allotted portion, quotas reduce the "noisy neighbour" problem, which occurs when one tenant adversely affects the productivity of other renters.

Kubernetes needs you to set resource requests and restrictions for each container when you apply a quota to the namespace. The maximum quantity of resources that a container can use is known as a limit. Depending on the type of resource, containers that try to use more than the configured limitations will either be throttled or destroyed. Each container is guaranteed the required amount when resource requests are set below restrictions, but there may still be some possibility for effect across workloads.

5.4.2 Network Segmentation and Traffic Isolation for Fault Containment

By default, all network communication in a Kubernetes cluster is unencrypted and all pods are permitted to connect with one another. When communication is unintentionally or maliciously directed to an unwanted location or is intercepted by a task on a compromised node, this might result in security issues.

Network Policies, which limit communication between pods using namespace labels or IP address ranges, can be used to manage pod-to-pod communication. Starting with a default policy that prohibits communication between pods and adding another rule that permits all pods to query the DNS server for name resolution is advised in multi-tenant environments where stringent network isolation between tenants is necessary. You can start implementing more lenient rules that permit communication within a namespace after you have such a default policy in place. Additionally, it is advised against using the empty label selector "{}" for namespace. If traffic between namespaces needs to be permitted, use the selector field in the network policy specification. As needed, this plan can be improved. Keep in mind that this only pertains to pods that are part of the same control plane; pods from separate virtual control planes are unable to communicate with one another using Kubernetes networking.

The development of default or common network policies may be made easier with the use of namespace management tools. Furthermore, some of these solutions enable you to enforce a uniform set of namespace labels throughout your cluster, guaranteeing that they serve as a reliable foundation for your policies.

A CNI plugin that facilitates network policy implementation is necessary. Network Policy resources will be disregarded otherwise.

Service meshes, which offer OSI Layer 7 regulations based on workload identification in addition to namespaces, may offer more sophisticated network isolation. When several namespaces are assigned to a single tenant, these higher-level policies can facilitate the management of namespace-based multi-tenancy. They often work across dedicated or virtual clusters and provide encryption using mutual TLS, safeguarding your data even in the presence of a compromised node. They might not be suitable for all users, though, and they might be much more difficult to administer.

5.4.3 Operational Governance and Isolation in Multi-Tenant Kubernetes Clusters

A cluster's computing, storage, networking, and control plane resources are shared by several tenants under the Kubernetes multi-tenancy architectural model. Multi-tenancy is a resource-sharing strategy where each tenant's data and workloads are conceptually segregated from one another.

Multi-tenancy is not a default feature of Kubernetes. Achieving secure and reliable multi-tenant architecture requires deliberate configuration of isolation boundaries to prevent interference, resource exhaustion, and unauthorized access between tenants.

Resource Isolation and Fair Allocation

In a multi-tenant cluster, workloads compete for shared resources such as CPU and memory. The absence of safeguards may permit a tenant to use the available resources above-average and poison the performance of other tenants - also known as the noisy neighbour's problem.

This is handled by Kubernetes using the Resource Quota object that restricts aggregate resource usage in a namespace. CPU, memory, and object quotas are allowed. With quotas on, users need to specify resource requests and limits to their workloads, so that resource allocation is predictable and resource monopolization is prevented.

Limit Ranges is used to supplement quotas with default and maximum resource constraints on each container. A combination of these mechanisms ensures equity in the distribution of resources and steady performance among tenants.

Access Isolation with RBAC

Authorization is very important in control plane isolation. In the case where tenants are capable of altering resources that are not within the scope of their intended purpose, they can circumvent other isolation mechanisms.

"Role-Based Access Control" (RBAC) is used to control actions performed by users or service accounts. The core RBAC objects are:

- **Role** (namespace-scoped permissions)
- **Cluster Role** (cluster-wide permissions)
- **Role Binding** (binds roles within a namespace)
- **Cluster Role Binding** (binds cluster-wide roles)

By mapping tenants to specific namespaces and restricting permissions using namespace-scoped roles, administrators enforce the **principle of least privilege**, ensuring tenants can manage only their own workloads.

Network Isolation

Kubernetes by default enables pod-to-pod unrestricted communication in a cluster. This action poses as a security risk in a multi-tenant environment.

Network Policies limit the traffic flow between pods with label selectors and namespace scopes. Another typical isolation strategy is default deny which starts with a default deny policy and only allows needed communication.

Due to the label-based policies, not an IP-based policy, the policies are dynamic to the resources created dynamically. Network isolation means that the workloads of tenants will not be able to accidentally or intentionally connect with other tenants.

Better Isolation with Virtual Clusters.

Namespace offers logical isolation, but does not offer total control plane isolation. There are resources that are shared among clusters.

Virtual clusters add a greater isolation boundary by implementing a virtualized Kubernetes control plane within an existing cluster. The virtual clusters have the capacity to incorporate virtual cluster-specific API server, controller manager, and storage abstraction, thus enjoying greater logical isolation but sharing the underlying infrastructure.

This will ensure a balance between cost-effectiveness and improved tenant isolation especially in settings that need a higher level of control.

Architectural Perspective

Multi-tenancy in Kubernetes is not a feature per se but rather a stacked isolation policy comprising of:

- Resource boundaries
- Access control boundaries
- Network segmentation
- Optional virtualized control planes

These layers allow resource sharing in a secure way without compromising the reliability and tenant autonomy, which is one of the prerequisites of building reliable cloud-native systems at scale. .

5.4.4 Node Isolation and Workload Placement Strategies

Another method for separating tenant workloads from one another is node isolation. Node isolation prevents tenant pods from co-mingling and dedicates a set of nodes to running pods from a certain tenant. Because every pod operating on a node will be a part of a single tenant, this architecture lessens the problem of noisy tenants. Because an attacker who escapes from a container will only have access to the containers and volumes mounted to that node, node isolation slightly reduces the risk of information leakage.

It is crucial to remember that the kubelet and, unless virtual control planes are being used, the API service are still shared services even though workloads from various tenants are operating on separate nodes. A competent attacker may move laterally within the cluster and access tenant workloads on other nodes by using the permissions granted to the kubelet or other pods operating on the node. If this is a significant issue, think about putting in place compensating controls like seccomp, AppArmor, or SELinux. You can also look at employing sandboxed containers or setting up distinct clusters for every tenant.

From a billing perspective, node isolation is slightly simpler than sandboxing containers because you can charge back per node instead of per pod. Additionally, compared to sandboxing containers, it may be simpler to create and has less compatibility and performance difficulties. For instance, each tenant's nodes can be set up with taints so that only pods with the appropriate tolerance can operate on them. Then, to ensure that pods launched into tenant namespaces operate on a particular set of nodes assigned to that tenant, a mutating webhook might be used to automatically add tolerations and node affinities.

5.5 Compliance and audit requirements

With the growth of Kubernetes use in various industries, organizations are being faced with a growing need to not only perform well in regard to operational reliability, but also in terms of regulatory compliance. Cloud-native systems usually handle sensitive information, cross jurisdictional, and maintain mission-critical services. Under those circumstances, compliance is not an incidental consideration but a building imperative. Kubernetes clusters are to be developed with governance, traceability, and verifiable controls embedded in them.

As opposed to conventional infrastructure, Kubernetes environments are very dynamic. The pods are created and destroyed automatically, the configurations are developed by CI/CD pipelines, and the workloads are scaled automatically. This dynamism creates the complexity of having a consistent security control and audit trail. In the absence of formal compliance systems, organizations are likely to experience configuration drift, lack of authorization, and regulatory non-compliance.

Auditability is the critical component of compliance that applies to cloud-native systems. The organizations should have the capability of answering the questions that are important: Who accessed the system? What changes were made? When did they occur? Regardless of the internal governance policies or external regulations like PCI DSS,

HIPAA, or GDPR, Kubernetes clusters should offer transparent logging, configuration management that can be traced and security policy that is enforced.

To architect reliable cloud-native systems, thus, compliance controls and audit controls need to be directly integrated into the Kubernetes control plane, the workload lifecycle, and deployment pipelines. To achieve operational agility and regulatory responsibility, Kubernetes can be used alongside logging, enforcing policies, role-based access control, and continuous validation to ensure that scalability is not compromised by governance.

5.5.1 Regulatory Frameworks and Kubernetes Compliance

Because it can manage and deploy containerised applications at scale, Kubernetes, an open-source container orchestration technology, has become very popular. As businesses use Kubernetes for their infrastructure, it becomes increasingly important to make sure that different governance and legal requirements are met. In Kubernetes, compliance entails following industry norms, security regulations, and domain-specific legal requirements.

The process of making sure that Kubernetes infrastructure and deployments adhere to relevant security and regulatory standards as well as organisational regulations is known as compliance. This entails taking charge of policies and security procedures to protect sensitive data, maintain appropriate access controls, and ensure the integrity and accessibility of Kubernetes-based applications.

Key Compliance Frameworks and Standards

There are a number of compliance frameworks and standards to use in the implementation of Kubernetes compliance. Commonly accepted frameworks are:

- **General Data Protection Regulation (GDPR)**: This is a regulation of the European Union, which defines the data protection and privacy standards of any organization that manages personal data of citizens of the EU.
- **Health Insurance Portability and Accountability Act (HIPAA):** This is the standard of protection of protected health information (PHI) within the healthcare sector in the United States.
- **Payment Card Industry Data Security Standard (PCI DSS)**: Standards that specify the requirements of data security of payment cards to avert fraud and other unscrupulous transactions during the payment processing.
- **National Institute of Standards and Technology (NIST) Cybersecurity Framework**: Incident provides a systematic framework in the management and enhancement of cybersecurity status of organizations.
- **ISO/IEC 27001**: A standard that is recognized internationally and specifies the best practice in creating, introducing, operating, and continuously enhancing an information security management system (ISMS).

These frameworks offer principles and control purposes that companies can embrace in order to attain compliance in Kubernetes settings.

Key Considerations for Kubernetes Compliance

Organizations must consider a number of issues to make Kubernetes compliant:

- **Secure Cluster Configuration:** Put in place secure settings in Kubernetes clusters, such as effective network segmentation, authentication, authorization policy, and encrypted data in transit and at rest.
- **Access Control:** Establish roles, role bindings and service accounts so that authorized users and applications can access only the resources of the cluster.

- **Container Security**: Make sure that container images are sound in security practices. Periodically scan and fix container images to detect vulnerabilities and track the runtime to detect threats.
- **Audit and Monitoring:** Introduce centralized logging and tracking in order to monitor activities in the Kubernetes environment. This assists in identifying security incidents, compliance violations and also aids in investigations.
- **Information Security**: Secure sensitive information with encryption of data at rest, in transit and backups. Store sensitive data like passwords, API keys and certificates using secure mechanisms.
- **Incident Response:** Draft and practice incident response plan with details of what should be done in the event of a security incident or compliance violation. Consistent checking and revision assists in providing effectiveness.

Supporting Technologies for Compliance

Kubernetes policy controllers can help organizations to impose compliance requirements and verify resource configurations against policy-based requirements. Security risks in container images can be determined by means of vulnerability scanning tools, and centralized logging and monitoring solutions will allow seeing the behaviour of the system and be audit-ready.

5.5.2 Audit Logging and Forensic Visibility

Cluster visibility is based on Kubernetes audit logs. They record who, what and when of user and service activity. Kubernetes audit logs are elaborate logs that capture every API server request, but important information captured includes:

- Who made the request
- When it occurred (timestamp)
- What resource was targeted (e.g., pod, service)

- Action taken (create, update, delete)
- Outcome of the request (success, failure)

Kubernetes includes built-in audit logging capabilities, but they are not enabled by default. In order to use audit logs, cluster administrators have to set up an audit policy containing what to log and install external tools to store, manage, and analyze the logs.

The Kubernetes logs also offer containers a contextual security with the identification of threats at the cluster orchestration level. But they do not observe processes and behaviour that are running within the containers, as Kubernetes runtime security does.

Both operations and security cannot do without audit logs, which provide actionable information on the activity of the cluster.

Components of Kubernetes Audit Logging

Kubernetes audit logs originate within the **kube-apiserver** component. Each time a user or process makes a request, an audit event is generated at every stage of the request's execution. The event is then processed based on a predefined audit policy and written to a backend. The audit policy specifies which events to log, while backends such as log files or webhooks manage the storage of these logs.

Audit policies define rules about which requests are recorded and what information each request needs to include. To set up an audit policy, teams must first record the parameters about the events that need to be logged. This includes defining which level of event needs to be recorded, which external storage needs to receive the log data, and the amount of time to retain log data.

Properly configuring the audit policy to store the right activity data and retain it for an appropriate length of time ensures that organizations can maximize the use of Kubernetes audit log data.

To analyze logs, DevOps and DevSecOps teams examine the structured JSON data within each log entry by looking for patterns or anomalies across the logs. The analysis typically involves using dedicated monitoring tools or "security information and event management" (SIEM) solutions to filter, query, and visualize the data to identify suspicious behavior or compliance issues.

When properly configured, audit policies can help a team to make sure that logs record the appropriate events with the level of detail required without including irrelevant noise and still capturing the important data. These logs, when used alongside effective analysis technology, including SIEM systems, are a formidable threat-detection tool, compliance-checking tool, and visibility-enhancing tool.

Kubernetes Audit Log Best Practices

Well-configured Kubernetes audit logs form a valuable basis of obtaining actionable insights, as well as staying secure and compliant. This can be done by establishing a properly outlined audit policy and selecting of the right storage backends.

An effective audit policy identifies:

- **Events to log:** Determined by matching rules.
- **Logging levels:** Options include:

    - **None:** Do not log events matching this rule.
    - **Metadata:** Log request metadata without the request or response body, such as user, timestamp, resource, and verb.
    - **Request:** Log metadata and the request body, excluding the response body.
    - **Request Response:** Log metadata, request, and response bodies.

A basic audit policy configuration may appear as follows:

```
Api Version: audit.k8s.io/v1
kind: Policy
rules:
  - level: RequestResponse
    omitStages:
      - RequestReceived
    resources:
      - group: “”
```

Additional field names like omit Stages can be used to avoid unnecessary stages (e.g. Request Received) to minimize noise to make the logs concerned with significant events.

Use External Storage for Secure and Scalable Log Retention

Audit logging operates on two levels:

- **Policy:** Determines which events are captured.
- **Backend:** Specifies how logs are stored or forwarded.

Audit log management requires external storage because storing logs in **etcd** is not supported for long-term retention. Instead:

- Use webhook backends or log forwarding tools to send logs to external storage.
- Configure retention policies to meet compliance requirements, which often require retaining logs for periods ranging from **two months to several years**.

External storage and centralized logging systems allow organizations to maintain scalable, secure log retention while supporting monitoring, forensic investigations, and regulatory compliance requirements.

5.5.3 Continuous Compliance and Policy Automation

Compliance and security controls in modern cloud native environments need to be active continuously and not conducted periodically using manual reviews. In Kubernetes environments, continuous compliance can be defined as the process of regularly verifying the infrastructure settings, workloads, and policies to be in line with the regulatory settings, organizational security policies, and operational best practices.

One of the tools to achieve the constant compliance is Policy as Code. Policy as code sets compliance requirements in executable code as opposed to documentation, enabling automated systems to check these requirements each time infrastructure changes happen. These checks are able to be executed during the execution of the CI/CD pipelines or Kubernetes admission or during infrastructure configuration changes and can ensure that the non-compliant configurations are identified before they can be deployed to production.

Automation of policies changes the conventional deploy first and verify later models to verify before deploy models. Automated policy analysis is used to make sure that only approved policy is deployed, and minimize the risk of misconfiguration, as well as assist in making environments compliant.

Policy enforcement is often implemented in Kubernetes using admission controllers, which make sense of API requests before resources are created or updated. These controllers compare deployment requests with laid down policies, and either approve or refuse the operation based on whether the operation satisfies the necessary security and compliance criteria.

There is a wide variety of policy engines that are typically used to automate compliance in Kubernetes environments. Open Policy Agent (OPA) can be used to define policies in a declarative form, and apply them to all of the clusters and infrastructure elements within Kubernetes. The security policies can be security rules like the limitation of privileged containers, obligatory labelling of resources, or that workloads are sourced to trusted registries of containers.

The Kubernetes resources are also integrated with other policy frameworks like Kyverno, which enable the administrators to formulate governance rules in Kubernetes-native YAML syntax. These policy engines are automated to validate and enforce policies; the workloads always follow the set organizational standards.

CI/CD pipelines and GitOps workflows have also been the focus of continuous compliance through policy validation. Organizations can find configurations violations at an early stage of the deployment process by placing automated policy checks into the development lifecycle. This kind of a shift-left approach can enable developers to address security and compliance issues during the deployment phase as well as improve security posture and operational efficiency.

It is possible that organizations can respond to automated governance mechanisms in order to monitor and continuously monitor the configurations of the cluster, detect policy violations, and generate compliance reports. It is an automated control mechanism that maintains Kubernetes environments to adhere to regulatory and internal security policies and facilitates scalability and agility of current cloud-native environments.

Multiple-Choice Questions (MCQs)

1. **What is the primary purpose of Kubernetes security architecture?**

   A) To improve application UI design
   B) To secure workloads, cluster components, and communication
   C) To increase pod startup speed
   D) To reduce container image size

2. **Which Kubernetes component is mainly responsible for enforcing authentication and authorization requests?**

   A) kube-proxy
   B) kubelet
   C) API Server
   D) CoreDNS

3. **In Kubernetes, which mechanism is commonly used for Identity and Access Management (IAM)?**

   A) Role-Based Access Control (RBAC)
   B) Horizontal Pod Autoscaler
   C) StatefulSets
   D) Ingress Controller

4. **What is the main purpose of RBAC in Kubernetes?**

   A) To balance traffic across services
   B) To control who can access resources and what actions they can perform
   C) To monitor node performance
   D) To automate pod scheduling

5. **Which Kubernetes feature helps enforce security and operational rules on workloads before they are created?**

A) Admission Controllers
B) ReplicaSets
C) Services
D) ConfigMaps

6. **Which of the following is an example of a policy enforcement mechanism in Kubernetes?**

A) Network Policies
B) Persistent Volumes
C) Deployments
D) Secrets Store CSI Driver

7. **What is the primary goal of multi-tenancy in Kubernetes?**

A) To run only one application per cluster
B) To allow multiple teams or workloads to securely share the same cluster
C) To reduce the number of nodes in a cluster
D) To replace namespaces with pods

8. **Which Kubernetes construct is most commonly used to provide logical isolation between teams or applications?**

A) Namespace
B) Container Runtime
C) Node Pool
D) DaemonSet

9. **Why are compliance and audit requirements important in Kubernetes environments?**

A) They help improve pod scheduling speed
B) They ensure regulatory adherence, traceability, and accountability

C) They replace encryption mechanisms
D) They eliminate the need for monitoring tools

10. Which Kubernetes feature is most useful for tracking who performed an action in the cluster?

A) Audit Logs
B) Service Accounts
C) ReplicaSets
D) Resource Quotas

Answer

1	2	3	4	5	6	7	8	9	10
B	C	A	B	A	A	B	A	B	A

Chapter 6

Kubernetes In Hybrid And Enterprise Environments

6.1 On-premises and Cloud Deployment Models

Kubernetes is now the default platform used to coordinate containerized applications on a variety of infrastructure platforms. With the modernization of the IT systems, organizations are making more and more use of Kubernetes in an environment that is a combination of cloud and data centre computing. This mixed strategy enables the companies to strike a balance between performance, scalability, cost-efficiency, and regulatory control and to retain control of critical workloads.

On premise deployments are still relevant in organizations where data control is imperative, low latency access to internal systems or where the organization must adhere to regulation policies which demand that information be processed and stored in particular locations. Operating Kubernetes on-premise data centre can allow organizations to gain access to direct control of infrastructure resources, as well as embrace modern container orchestration. Such environments tend to be complementary to current virtualization platforms, storage systems and internal networking structures.

Instead, public cloud environments offer very flexible and controlled infrastructure that makes the process of implementing and running Kubernetes much easier. Major cloud providers offer managed Kubernetes services, which automate the process of cluster provisioning, upgrades, scaling, and infrastructure maintenance. This will enable development groups to dedicate more time to application delivery and less time to operational workload to operate Kubernetes clusters.

Practically, most organizations have a hybrid deployment system that integrates on-premise infrastructure with cloud-based Kubernetes systems. Hybrid architectures also allow enterprises to execute sensitive workloads in the local environment without sacrificing elasticity of cloud resources to burst workloads, development environments, and to provide services across the globe. This elastic deployment model contributes to the current cloud-native architectures, as well as to enterprise operational and regulatory restrictions.

6.1.1 On-Premises Kubernetes Deployments

Instead of outsourcing infrastructure to cloud providers, Kubernetes on-premises refers to the implementation of Kubernetes clusters inside an organization's physical data centers. This method runs containerised apps on the company's current hardware and network infrastructure. Complete control over the environment, including hardware, networks, and storage systems, is possible with on-premises Kubernetes.

Certain corporate needs, such data sovereignty or regulatory compliance, can be satisfied by implementing Kubernetes internally. It provides the flexibility to construct an architecture that closely adheres to security standards and organisational regulations. Organisations that have made significant investments in data centre resources or that want a high degree of control over their workloads will find this arrangement especially helpful.

Nonetheless, Kubernetes on-premise deployment has its own challenges. Kubernetes is a complicated system that cannot be deployed and operated without specific knowledge. Also, when an organization implements Kubernetes on-premises, it becomes the full provider of purchasing, maintaining, or scaling the hardware which it is implemented on.

Benefits of Running Kubernetes On-Premises

- **Compliance and Data Privacy**

On-premise Kubernetes supports strict regulatory and data privacy laws. It enables organizations to impose compliance criteria and information control policies directly. The general control of data stored and handled in the physical premises has given the businesses some level of control, thus they are able to control the compliance with the legal and operational regulations.

On-premises deployments are also very important in minimizing threats posed by data breach and external attacks. The physical security of the infrastructure is an additional security layer, which is essential in such industries as finance, healthcare, and government where there is a high priority on the protection of sensitive data.

- **Cloud Agnostic Setup**

On-premise Kubernetes supports strict regulatory and data privacy laws. It enables organizations to impose compliance criteria and information control policies directly. The general control of data stored and handled in the physical premises has given the businesses some level of control, thus they are able to control the compliance with the legal and operational regulations.

On-premises deployments are also very important in minimizing threats posed by data breach and external attacks. The physical security of the infrastructure is an additional security layer, which is essential in such industries as finance, healthcare, and government where there is a high priority on the protection of sensitive data.

- **Cost**

In case organizations have available data centre resources, on-premises Kubernetes can prove to be cheaper than using cloud resources. It also leverages on internal infrastructure to reduce the cost of running operations on the cloud. Hardware and configuration may require initial cost in case it will pay off in the long run, particularly when the workload is large or continuous.

Cost advantages however are based on internal competency and management effectiveness of in-house resources. Companies should thoroughly consider their ability to sustain and expand Kubernetes systems with the operational needs and possible cost reductions.

Challenges of On-Premises Kubernetes

Implementing Kubernetes on-premise may also lead to a number of major issues to organizations.

- **No Outsourced Management**

On-prem K8s deployment reduces the reliance on cloud providers, moving the workload to an in-house setup. Although this provides control, it involves a dedicated effort in terms of monitoring, updating and securing of the infrastructure. Contrary to the cloud services, where the vendors are in charge of the underlying platform, organizations have the overall stack, which requires specific teams to maintain the stack and address any issues.

- **Hardware: Hardware is owned by different departments that share responsibility.**

Physical hardware is another important issue to manage in the on-premises setups. Organisations have to deal with procurement and installation, maintenance and subsequent upgrades or replacements. This involves up-capital outlay and a permanent operating cost. The failure of hardware may be a source of downtime, and additional complexity and planning are required to scale resources to satisfy demand.

- **Networking Complexity**

Kubernetes networking is a difficult thing, and it takes a special effort to install it on premises, whereas on the cloud, it is usually configured. This includes set up and administration of internal networks, load balancers, firewalls, and even integrating with already existing IT infrastructure. High availability, security and optimal performance require specific expertise and constant monitoring.

- **Persistent Storage**

To handle persistent storage in an on-premise Kubernetes setup, specific attention must be paid to choosing the storage solutions that can be dynamically provisioned, be highly available, and have a disaster recovery mechanism. The organizations also need to provide accessibility and data integrity within the Kubernetes cluster; at the same time keeping the performance at par with the need to stay cost effective and scaleable.

6.1.2 Managed Kubernetes in Public Clouds

Managed Kubernetes services are cloud solutions that are offered as a fully managed Kubernetes environment where organizations can easily deploy and manage their containerized application. These services eliminate much of the complexities that come with configuring and operating a Kubernetes cluster, as the organizations do not need to worry about configuring hardware or operating the control plane. This liberates the precious time and allows teams to work more on application development and innovation. Load balancing, storage, networking, and monitoring capabilities are also taken care of by managed services.

The major advantages of operating managed Kubernetes services are:

- **Less operational complexity:** Cloud providers do the provisioning, scaling and maintenance of Kubernetes clusters, and organizations no longer have to deal with underlying infrastructure.
- **Scalability without interruption:** Managed Kubernetes services provide automatic scaling solutions, which enable an organization to automatically scale up or down applications according to the demands.
- **Strong security:** Cloud providers practice security and frequently release security patches and features to their managed Kubernetes services.

Amazon Elastic Kubernetes Service (EKS)

Amazon "Elastic Kubernetes Service" (EKS) is a managed Kubernetes service offered by AWS which is a highly available and scalable Kubernetes environment hosted on the AWS cloud. EKS clusters can be used to handle high and stable workloads, which are provided by functionalities like automatic version upgrades and the ability to choose types of powerful EC2 instances. EKS also has "identity access management" (IAM) to authenticate users and integrates with multiple services including Amazon "Elastic Container Registry" (ECR), Amazon CloudWatch, and AWS networking services.

The major characteristics and advantages of EKS are:

- **Integration with the AWS services:** EKS is integrated with the AWS networking, monitoring as well as security services to facilitate the deployment and operations of the application.
- **High availability and scalability:** EKS spreads control plane components to different Availability Zones to ensure availability.
- **Security and compliance features**: IAM integration, network isolation and encryption mechanisms can be used to secure applications and cluster resources.

Azure Kubernetes Service (AKS)

Azure Kubernetes Service (AKS): Microsoft managed Kubernetes service is a highly available Kubernetes environment provided by Azure in its cloud system. AKS also makes it easy to deploy and run containerized applications, which means that an organization does not need to take care of the infrastructure components but can build and deliver applications.

The major characteristics and advantages of AKS are:

- **Integration with the Azure services:** Azure Kubernetes services can be integrated with Microsoft Entra ID (previously Azure Active Directory), Azure Container Registry, Azure Monitor, and Azure Policy.
- **Streamlined cluster operations and scaling:** AKS is an automated Kubernetes cluster provisioning and scaling and maintenance.
- **Security** functions: secure deployments can be executed with integration with identity services, role-based access control (RBAC), and network policies.

Google Kubernetes Engine (GKE)

Google Cloud offers a managed Kubernetes service called Google Kubernetes Engine (GKE), which is essentially a fully managed, highly available Kubernetes environment.

Numerous operational facets of running Kubernetes clusters, such as load balancing, networking, scalability, and cluster upgrades, are managed by GKE.

GKE's salient characteristics and advantages include:

- **Integration with Google Cloud services:** Google Cloud Storage, Google Cloud Logging, and Google Cloud Monitoring are among the services that GKE interfaces with.
- **Automated operations and scalability:** GKE automates cluster provisioning, scaling, and maintenance.

- **Advanced security features:** Integration with identity and access management systems, network policies, and security controls helps protect workloads and cluster resources.

By lowering operational overhead and offering scalable, secure, and highly available services, managed Kubernetes services make it easier to install and operate Kubernetes clusters infrastructure for running containerized applications. Organizations adopting managed Kubernetes services can focus more on application development and delivery while leveraging the operational capabilities of cloud platforms.

6.1.3 Hybrid Kubernetes Architecture

Kubernetes hybrid cloud is gaining traction as organizations seek to balance the benefits of on-premise infrastructure with the flexibility of the public cloud. It entails the implementation and management of applications in a mix of environments, which will result in a single system. This strategy is more flexible and has the possibility of cost optimization, yet it brings management problems.

The Architecture of Kubernetes Hybrid Cloud

On-premise infrastructure and public cloud resources managed by Kubernetes are commonly combined in a Kubernetes hybrid cloud architecture. While public cloud resources give flexibility, on-premise infrastructure offers dedicated resources. Network connectivity and security are crucial for these components to interact effectively.

The architecture generally includes the following components:

- **On-Premise Infrastructure:** supplies the networking, storage, and physical servers needed to host containerised apps.
- **Public Cloud Resources:** Provides networking, storage, and processing power as needed.
- **Kubernetes Control Plane:** Consists of the API server, scheduler, controller manager, etcd, and other components that oversee and coordinate deployments across environments.

- **Network connectivity:** Provides safe connection between cloud and on-premise environments.

Workload portability is made possible by Kubernetes hybrid cloud, which permits apps to switch between on-premise and cloud environments without requiring major code modifications. Applications and their dependencies are packed together thanks to containerisation, which facilitates their deployment across various infrastructures.

Different Methods for creating hybrid Kubernetes environments consist of:

- **VPNs:** Create secure tunnels between on-premise networks and cloud infrastructure.
- **Direct Connections:** Provide dedicated network links with reduced latency and increased bandwidth.
- **Service Meshes:** These offer a layer of abstraction to control communication between services in different settings.

Networking and Connectivity in Hybrid Environments

Networking plays a critical role in Kubernetes hybrid cloud environments by enabling communication between on-premise and cloud systems. Secure and reliable connectivity is necessary to ensure that applications function correctly across different infrastructures.

Common connectivity approaches include:

- **VPNs (Virtual Private Networks):** VPNs provide safe connections between on-premise and cloud networks by building encrypted tunnels across the open internet.
- **Direct Connections:** Dedicated network connections such as AWS Direct Connect or Azure ExpressRoute provide greater bandwidth, lower latency, and more dependable performance.

Routing rules and network policies are crucial for safe communication. While routing rules control how traffic moves between services and infrastructure components, network policies specify how pods communicate with one another. Isolating workloads and preventing unwanted access are two benefits of proper configuration.

Workload Portability and Service Meshes

Kubernetes makes workloads portable between hybrid environments because it is an abstracted application on the underlying infrastructure. Containerization takes applications and dependencies and packages them into portable containers such that they can execute in various environments. Kubernetes then coordinates these containers through deployment, scaling and networking.

In hybrid environments, service to service communication and security can be enhanced by service meshes. A service mesh is a service infrastructure layer that can provide communication between services and may offer functionality like control of traffic, authentication, authorization, and observability.

Benefits and Use Cases of Kubernetes Hybrid Cloud

There are various advantages of having a Kubernetes hybrid cloud approach.

- **Greater Resilience:** Hybrid deployments are redundant and have failover. In the event of an outage of one of the environments, there is the possibility of the workloads moving to another environment.
- **Increased Resource Rationalization:** Organizations are able to allocate workloads according to demand, deploying cloud resources at times of high demand and ensuring a minimum level of workloads in premises.
- **Enhanced Application Performance**: Applications can execute in an environment that is most appropriate to their needs like running latency sensitive applications on-premise and scalable cloud services.

The hybrid Kubernetes environments have common applications such as disaster recovery, burst capacity in peak workloads, and edge computing applications where data processing takes place nearer to where the data are available.

Kubernetes hybrid cloud provides a unified platform for managing applications across multiple environments. This allows organizations to deploy and scale applications efficiently while optimizing infrastructure resources and maintaining flexibility in their deployment strategies.

6.2 Migration patterns and anti-patterns

With the use of Kubernetes to modernize infrastructure, the challenge of migrating the existing application and workloads is critical as organizations are adopting the technology. A lot of businesses use complicated systems, which initially were designed to support both traditional monolithic and virtual machines. The migration of these systems to Kubernetes can be done only after planning and evaluating architecture and getting familiar with proper migration strategies. Organizations can experience the breakdown of operations, performance, or additional complexity of the system without an organized migration strategy.

Ketos can hardly be migrated in one step. Rather, organizations are more likely to undergo gradual transition strategies that enable the organization to keep running with existing applications as new cloud-native features are brought up. There are various migration patterns with respect to the application architecture, operational constraints and long term modernization objectives. Certain applications may be migrated with few changes whereas some of them may need deeper architectural changes to take full advantage of Kubernetes benefits such as container orchestration, scalability and automated resource management.

Simultaneously, companies should be sensitive to the typical migration anti-patterns that may negatively affect the advantages of adopting Kubernetes. The desire to treat Kubernetes as an immediate substitute of the conventional infrastructure without modifying application construction and operation methodologies usually results in a inefficient implementation and management issues. Poor observability, a lack of automation, and poorly configured containerization strategies may make matters operational rather than make them easier to manage.

Awareness of effective migration patterns and also of possible anti-patterns allows organizations to make quality decisions during the process of migrating into Kubernetes environments. With the utilization of organized migration approaches and pitfalls elimination, businesses may steadily modernize their application platform without losing dependability, execution, and stability in the process.

6.2.1 Lift-and-Shift Migration to Kubernetes

Lift and shift is known for its simplicity and speed, as it involves minimal changes to the existing application structure. It is the more common method of achieving applications migration to the cloud and is reflected to be a cheaper initial solution. Initially, lift and shift was mostly employed to replicate on-premises applications in the cloud dimension. Nevertheless, this strategy saves the expenses and resources needed to redesign everything; however, it can be counterproductive to utilize the cost benefits and functionality of cloud-native infrastructure, including autoscaling.

Lift and shift can be viewed in the wider context of the digital transformation as a step towards organizations that are going to enter cloud computing with the first steps. It offers a place where businesses have begun to realize the benefits of cloud quickly, but it might need further optimization or re-developing to be more molded to cloud-specific capabilities and efficiencies. The approach is especially useful when the pattern to be migrated is easy to define or when the business requires a solution that will allow the migration within limited time limitations.

Key Benefits of Lift and Shift

The lift and shift cloud migration strategy has a number of major advantages to businesses migrating to cloud and each of them adds to the efficiency of the entire migration procedure.

Cost Savings

- **Less Infrastructure Cost:** Removes the physical server maintenance cost, and lowers hardware costs and operational cost.
- **Efficient use of resources**: Pay per usage of the cloud resources, and it results in improved cost management.
- **Reduced start up cost:** Little modification to applications will lower the cost of migration at the start up.

Speed and Simplicity

- **Shorter Migration Schedule**: Moving the existing applications directly accelerates the migration.
- **Simplicity of implementation:** This one does not demand so much technical skills and planning as an entire application overhaul.

Minimal Disruption

- **Business Continuity:** Allows ongoing operations to run without significant downtime.
- **Familiarity in Operations:** Employees continue using the same applications, reducing the learning curve and adaptation time.

Potential Limitations

As much as lift and shift is an advantageous migration strategy, it is associated with a number of challenges.

Interoperability and Performance.

- **Potential Integration Problems:** There are the possible on-premises applications that might not be compatible with the new environment.

- **Performance Variances:** There may be no performance without some optimization.

Strategies to address these include thorough testing and performance monitoring to identify and resolve compatibility and efficiency issues.

Lack of Cloud-Native Utilization

- **Limited Use of Cloud Features:** Lift and shift migrations may not fully leverage cloud-native functionalities such as scalability and flexibility.
- **Future Redevelopment Needs:** Applications may require future re-architecting to optimize platform capabilities.

To address these challenges, organizations often plan a phased approach in which the initial lift and shift migration is followed by gradual integration of cloud-native features and re-architecting as needed. Careful planning and evaluation ensure that the lift and shift approach aligns with long-term business goals and migration strategies.

6.2.2 Refactoring and Cloud-Native Migration Approaches

The cloud migration refactoring process involves the restructuring of an existing application to make it cloud-ready. This migration type differs from "lift and shift," where a business transfers data and assets to a cloud storage facility without changes or modifications.

Cloud refactoring can involve the following actions:

- Redesign or optimize code
- Change the architecture to accommodate new scaling abilities
- Enhance security and data privacy measures
- Replat form the application to make it cloud-compatible

Benefits of Refactoring for Cloud Migration

Refactoring is a powerful approach that allows businesses to gain several advantages during the cloud migration journey, although it requires technical skills and adds extra time to the migration process.

- **Improved longevity:** Refactoring helps companies preserve legacy software. The process often simplifies code and makes it easier to maintain and update in the future.
- **Improved application performance and scalability:** By restructuring code, organizations can significantly enhance application performance and scalability.
- **Increased cost efficiency:** Applications use existing resources more effectively, which can lead to cost savings over time.
- **Increased security and compliance:** Applications may be re-engineered in order to meet data privacy policy and offer better security in the cloud.
- **Better user experience**: Refactoring may offer an improved user experience and make an application remain competitive.

Challenges of Refactoring During Cloud Migration

Despite the numerous advantages associated with refactoring, the process also presents some challenges to the organizations that should be taken into account during the process of migration.

- **Time-consuming process:** Refactoring can be complicated and it can add more time and cost to the overall migration.
- **Expertise deficiency:** It needs advanced technical skills to alter and debug application code.
- **Technical risk:** Refactoring can result in unstable or unreliable applications because of errors introduced in the refactoring process.
- **Unexpected problems:** Refactoring can help identify undetected deficiencies of the current application structure that were not apparent before.
- **Vendor lock-in:** Refactoring can introduce a dependency on particular cloud services or platforms, which can be more challenging to move to in the future.

When organizations restructure their applications to match cloud-native architectures, they can enhance their scalability, maintainability, long-term operational efficiency as well as modernizing the application environment.

6.2.3 Incremental and Hybrid Migration Strategies

The modernization of legacy application is a big challenge to organizations that aim at holding their businesses afloat and still incorporate new modern architectures and technologies. The dangers of total system rewrites usually prevent the advantages of doing so, and a strong argument in favour of incremental migration strategies exists. Incremental strategy helps the organization to modernize at a manageable rate without interfering with essential business.

Legacy applications can contain years of business logic, workflow and processes. Also, these systems often are at the backbone of the operations of organizations, hence replacement them being a risky undertaking. Conventional methods of legacy replacement have frequently been based on the use of a big bang migration, meaning that the whole system is rewritten and replaced simultaneously. The complexity of replacing key systems is likely to result in high failure rates, budget overruns and deadlines missed in such projects.

Incremental approaches are more sustainable as they offer the modernization process more manageable bits each offering tangible value. Organizations modernize one component or service at a time rather than migrate a whole application simultaneously. This will enable teams to check their migration strategies, system performance and modify their approach according to the results of previous phases of the migration.

CIM Strategies Nuclear Incremental Migration Strategies.

There are a number of strategies that allow organizations to modernize the legacy systems slowly without interruption of operations.

1. **Strangler Fig Pattern**

The strangler fig design gives a gradual process of the replacement of the old functionality without having the system to a halt. New elements are constructed over the old application and certain functionality is slowly assigned to the new implementations. During the increase in the modern components, additional traffic is directed to them until the legacy system can be finally decommissioned.

2. **Encapsulation Strategy**

Encapsulation is the process of enveloping the legacy system by a modern interface layer that prevents the new applications with the details of the legacy implementation. Modern APIs are traditionally exposed with API facades and communicate internally with the legacy system. This has the advantage of enabling new applications to be compatible with legacy systems without compromising existing functionality.

3. **Decomposition Approach**

Monolithic systems that are in use can be disaggregated into small and manageable parts. The system has functional boundaries that are determined and individual components are separated and modernized separately. This divide and conquer strategy allows teams to modernize the most essential elements first and preserve the integrity of the system, in general.

4. **Parallel Implementation**

Parallel implementation implies the creation of a new version of a particular functionality as the legacy implementation still runs. Both implementations could occur parallel to each other during a validation stage to see that the new system works as it should. After confirming the new implementation, the traffic is thus gradually redirected to the modern system as opposed to the legacy system.

Incremental and hybrid migration strategies enable the organizations to modernize the complex systems and minimize the risk of the operations. Enterprises can move towards cloud-native systems like containerized applications and Kubernetes-based systems by gradually replacing legacy systems with modern ones and keeping interoperability but ensuring stability as they do so.

6.2.4 Common Kubernetes Migration Anti-Patterns

Anti-pattern is a dangerous approach to what is generally an ineffective solution to a problem. On the surface, such kinds of solutions seem to be correct and efficient. Nevertheless, the benefits of such patterns are usually temporary, and the outcomes of the anti-patterns prove to be more problematic than they are worth.

In the situation where the developer decides to adopt an anti-pattern, it is normally with the view of making some future corrections. In reality, this is never usually the case, as other priorities prevail. Breaking best-practice design patterns introduces technical debt, which finally has to be settled by refactoring or the technical instability and downtime costs of the system.

Kubernetes also has anti-patterns. The Kubernetes orchestration systems are structured to handle cloud-native workloads that are based on elasticity, fault tolerance, and architectures that are distributed. The transfer of the legacy system or the creation of the distributed systems without proper planning may spread various anti-patterns that will lower the reliability and efficiency of working processes.

- **Lack of Health Checks**

Health checks are used to provide systems with a means of validating the status of services and verifying that applications are correctly running. They aid in establishing details like the availability of services, system performance and connection with other services that it relies on. Kubernetes has a set of container probes, including liveness Probe, readiness Probe, and startup Probe, which allow services to be monitored and recovered automatically. Applications cannot make full use of self-healing capabilities offered by Kubernetes without health monitoring.

- **Failure to use Blue/green or Canary Deployment models.**

Strategies in deployment are essential when keeping the application available at an update. Kubernetes allows deployment strategies Recreate and Rolling Update. Nevertheless, such strategies might be restricted, e.g. downtime during deployment or more advanced rollback processes.

On a more sophisticated deployment strategy, blue-green deployments and canary deployments enable safer application updates release. Blue-green deployment implements two versions of a service running at the same time so that, only with validation can traffic move to the new version. Canary deployment works by slowly diverting a low percentage of traffic to the new version as it checks the behaviour of the system. Lack of such methods can increase the risk of service disruption in updates to the application.

- **Not Using Circuit Breakers**

Network calls used between services are common in distributed systems that are implemented using Kubernetes. Since such services can operate across various nodes, such calls can fail either because of network latency, resource overload, or service failures. Circuit breakers keep track of service interactions and interrupt requests to failing services after a problem has been identified. This avoids failures in different parts of the system and enables the platform to redirect traffic to available healthy service instances.

- **Failing to Gather Sufficient Metrics.**

Observability is a necessary factor in the behaviour of systems in distributed settings. Metrics contain data concerning the performance of the service, the utilization of resources and the health of the system.

In case of inadequate metrics gathering, it is challenging to point out problems in performance, detect failures, or troubleshoot problems. With the level of complexity of systems, it becomes necessary to get metrics of numerous services and components to ensure the reliability and performance of the systems.

Knowledge of these generic anti-patterns assists organizations to circumvent migration errors and establish Kubernetes configurations that are robust, observable, and that comply with cloud-native architectural standards.

6.3 Governance and compliance models

The governance and compliance models are essential to enterprise Kubernetes environments, particularly when the organizations work in various teams, regions, and regulatory environments. With the prevalence of Kubernetes in the corporate sector, it has become crucial to maintain uniformity in the standards of operation, security measures and policy implementation to govern sophisticated cloud-native infrastructure. Governance structures assist in specifying the manner in which the Kubernetes resources are availed, accessed, and managed throughout the organization.

Enterprise governance in Kubernetes cluster guarantees that organizational policies regarding security, access control, resource usage, and operational procedures are adhered to in Kubernetes clusters. With the lack of adequate governance mechanisms, organizations can experience the following problems: an uncontrolled use of resources, unstable configurations, security risks, and the inability to ensure operational stability in a variety of clusters and teams.

Compliance, conversely, is concerned with the fact that the Kubernetes instantiations are compliant with the regulatory, industry, and in-house organizational policies. Most industries, such as finance, health care and even the government sectors have stringent regulatory frameworks which demand a high level of control over data protection, access control, auditing, and transparency of operations.

Governance and compliance models of Kubernetes thus represent the integration of policy enforcement, monitoring, access control systems, and audit features to ensure that cloud-native systems run securely, efficiently and in line with the requirements of the regulatory requirements. Through regulated governance patterns, business organizations will be able to ensure a consistent state of operations, prevent security threats, and keep Kubernetes setups in line with internal policies and regulatory bodies.

6.3.1 Organizational Policy Management in Kubernetes Environment

Kubernetes provides a declarative management interface. Users can specify the desired state of the system using API definitions, and Kubernetes controllers then work to make the current state match the desired state. This approach is used for managing cluster nodes and services as well as for managing application workloads.

A policy typically represents required configurations. Kubernetes itself provides several policies such as:

- **Network Policies:** to secure network traffic to and from pods
- **Pod Security Standards:** to control privilege and access profiles for pods
- **Quotas and Limit Range:** to manage resource utilization and fairness

These Kubernetes policies are native API objects that govern the behavior of the Kubernetes cluster. However, there are several situations where users want to configure settings that are required cluster-wide and even across clusters within an enterprise. These Kubernetes constructs are powerful but have no effect if not configured. Configuring them correctly for multiple workloads is also a non-trivial task.

For successful adoption and growth of enterprise Kubernetes, an organizational pattern that is emerging is the formation of an internal platform team responsible for managing Kubernetes clusters, the underlying infrastructure, and the common services that must run in each cluster or be shared across clusters. These services are required to operationalize Kubernetes and may include monitoring, logging, security, backup, and disaster recovery.

The platform team provides Kubernetes services and solutions to product development teams within the enterprise. The platform team is also responsible for setting Kubernetes policies for the security and proper configuration and operation of clusters and workloads. For example, platform teams may mandate that resource quotas are required on all shared clusters.

To scale Kubernetes usage effectively, it is necessary that a central team is responsible for ensuring proper configuration of Kubernetes policies and validation of best-practice guidelines. This is why Kubernetes policy management is becoming increasingly important for enterprise Kubernetes.

Kubernetes is designed to be extended using Custom Resources. Custom Resources allow the introduction of new object types that can be managed through the Kubernetes API. For example, custom resources can be specified in YAML files and managed using standard Kubernetes tools such as Customize.

The Custom Resource mechanism allows Kubernetes to be extended while utilizing common tooling for managing Kubernetes configurations. Policy management is a form of configuration management where a policy provides defaults for configuration and determines what is allowed or disallowed. Therefore, it is important that a Kubernetes policy management solution adopts the same practices and approach used for Kubernetes management.

Kubernetes policy management plays an important role in enabling consistent governance across clusters and workloads in enterprise environments. Organizations increasingly require mechanisms that allow policies to be defined, managed, and enforced using Kubernetes-native approaches that integrate naturally with existing Kubernetes configuration and deployment workflows.

6.3.2 Resource Governance and Quota Management

Resource competition can be an issue when more than one team uses shared Kubernetes resources. Without good controls, one application can occupy the resources in the cluster, therefore, reducing the performance of all the workloads. The effective management of these resources is thus a significant task of cluster administrators particularly when there are numerous workloads running on the same infrastructure as in enterprise contexts.

Kubernetes offers the administrator with the means to manage resource consumption via the Resource Quota object. Resource quotas are Kubernetes resources that offer constraints to aggregate resource consumption in a namespace. They assist administrators to regulate the use of resources in a multi-tenant environment and to allocate cluster resources evenly between teams and applications.

Resource quotas are namespace level and provide hard limits of the aggregate resource consumption in that namespace. After a quota has been specified, Kubernetes implements it by refusing the creation of resources that exceed the specified limits. This control is done when creating the resource ensuring that workloads fall within the defined resource limits and that resource usage is not uncontrolled.

Kubernetes has various resource quotas that accommodate various facets of resource management in the cluster. Compute resource quotas are used to regulate the allocation of CPU and memory by restricting resource requests and resource limits to aid in the equitable allocation of computational resources. Storage quotas control perennial storage resources by controlling the aggregate storage capacity that may be requested, the quantity of persistent volume claims, or use of particular storage classes. Object count quotas are used to limit the number of Kubernetes resources in a namespace, including pods, services, configmaps, secrets, and persistent volume claims, which can assist in preventing the unlimited creation of objects and controlling resources in the cluster.

Besides resource quotas, Kubernetes also offers Limit range objects which specify default and maximum resources allowed by a container and pod in a namespace. Although resource quotas are described as the aggregate consumption of resources on the namespace level, Limit Range objects are used to impose limits and defaults on per-container consumption. This way, every workload would state the right resource requests and resource limits so that quota enforcement becomes predictable and efficient.

The use of quotas is also a key element of resource governance that needs to be monitored. Administrators have access to the Kubernetes API, command-line tooling, and monitoring to know which resources are being used. The utilization of quotas can be observed to find the namespaces where the limits might be exceeded, and the administrators can respond by setting up policies or resources allocations before workloads start to fail because of quota limitations.

Resource governance is more essential as Kubernetes environments increase in size and more teams are utilizing the same infrastructure. Corrected quotas and resource policies assist in eliminating resource monopolization, keeping the system predictable, and ensuring equitable resource distribution among teams and workloads in enterprise Kubernetes settings.

6.3.3 Compliance Monitoring and Audit Traceability

Kubernetes being a container orchestration platform does not only handle the applications but also provides security and transparency in the operation of applications. Audit logs monitoring is one of the key Kubernetes governance aspects. Audit logs offer a chronological record of activities that transpire in a Kubernetes cluster that gives visibility to security-related incidents, configuration modifications, as well as operational activities.

Kuber audit logs are detailed logs of cluster events and interactions. These logs follow API interaction by capturing all the requests that are sent to the Kubernetes API server. The information in each log entry includes the identity of the person who sent the request, operation requested, and response of the server. It is useful to the administrators to understand the interaction between the users and applications with the cluster and gives the administrators a thorough insight into the activities going on within the system.

Security monitoring is also supported by audit logs because through audit logs, an administrator can be able to detect abnormal patterns that could be signs of security threats. Through such logs, one can monitor unauthorized access attempts, unusual changes of resources, or abnormal user activity, and therefore identify them. Audit logs are also monitored to monitor role, permission and resource configuration changes that are significant in safeguarding cluster security and operational stability.

The other important role that Kubernetes audit logs play is compliance checking. Various industries have stringent regulatory policies that force the organization to keep elaborate documentation of activities occurring in the system. Audit logs give written records that the cluster operations are within the organizational policies and regulations. These may be referred to when conducting compliance audits to prove that security controls, the access management policies, and the operational procedures are being adhered to.

Audit logs are of importance to the problem of troubleshooting and forensic analysis. The chronological record of events assists the administrators to determine the pace of events that resulted in the problem when there are issues with the operations. Audit logs, in case of security breach, offer a chronological and detailed record of the activity in the cluster, which assists the investigator in determining how the breach happened and what resources it impacted.

Audit log monitoring and analysis thus assists organizations to keep the operations visible and accountable within Kubernetes environments. Through audit record consultation and incorporating it into monitoring and analysis systems, administrators can identify suspicious activity, investigate incidences, and ensure that Kubernetes clusters are functioning as per the stipulated governance and compliance standards.

6.3.4 Enterprise Governance Automation and Policy Standardization

Kubernetes governance is a collection of policies, processes, and practices applicable to the management and utilization of Kubernetes environments in an organization. It provides a secure, efficient, and conforming operation of Kubernetes clusters. Governance is also significant in organizations that embrace Kubernetes since it offers a guideline on how to handle the complexity and risks involved in the deployment of Kubernetes. This lack of proper governance can result in issues in the security, compliance, poor handling of resources, and high cost of operation, unseen and uncontrollable in organizations.

There are various fundamental principles in Kubernetes governance to make sure that the Kubernetes environments are operated efficiently to serve business purposes. Such principles are security, compliance, cost control, resource optimization, and standardization. Security It is the practice of securing clusters and applications against unauthorized access and other threats. Compliance is concerned with regulatory compliance and industry compliance. Cost management and resource optimization allow using cluster resources efficiently and standardization can be used to create a consistent set of practices when deploying and managing Kubernetes workloads.

Enterprise Kubernetes governance is significant in the process of standardization. Standardizing naming, creating standard deployment templates, and having central repositories of Kubernetes manifestations can assist organizations to achieve consistency across groups and clusters. Standard policies and settings simplify the operation process and can be more readily used to control a large Kubernetes setup.

Another significant thing about governance is policy enforcement. Organizations should establish and implement policies that are consistent with the regulatory standards and the internal operation standards. Some tools like Open Policy Agent (OPA) enable administrators to write policies in the form of code, and assess the policies against requests sent to the Kubernetes API server. When compliance requirements are mapped against Kubernetes governance policies, organizations can be confident that Kubernetes environments comply with regulatory policies and internal security policies.

Governance policies need to be done at scale through automation. Automation helps in cutting down labour in the governance processes as well as enhancing uniformity in the implementation of policies. Insecure configurations can be prevented and resource constraints enforced alongside enforcement of defined standards by automated policy enforcing mechanisms before resources are deployed in the cluster. Compliance checks and monitoring processes based on automation can also be used to identify governance violations and send alerts when policies are not adhered to.

These are further enhanced by constant checking and auditing that augment governance practices in Kubernetes environments. Audit logs and monitoring tools give information about the use of resources, application performance, and security logs throughout the cluster.

Administrators can use audit logs and system behaviour to identify suspicious activities and ensure that governance policies are adhered to, as well as keep track of the behaviour of systems in a cluster environment.

With policy standardization, automated governance, and ongoing monitoring, enterprises may ensure that operational practices across multiple Kubernetes environments are consistent. These governance features assist organizations to impose security and compliance demands, optimally resource utilization, and effectively and dependable Kubernetes infrastructures in hybrid and enterprise deployments.

6.4 Organizational adoption challenges

As the adoption of Kubernetes has been on the rise among business enterprises, various challenges are normally presented to the organization during the process of adopting Kubernetes in the existing operational ecosystem. Even though Kubernetes has excellent capabilities of container orchestration, scalability and automation, the effective implementation of the technology in large organizations requires significant process, infrastructure management practices, and organization cultures change. The technical and operational issues should be put in mind by businesses to ensure that Kubernetes implementations can yield expected returns.

One of the core challenges of Kubernetes adoption is a change in the workflow and responsibility. Traditional IT settings tend to be constructed around a definite structure and with centralized management behavior, whereas Kubernetes settings are grounded on a significant level of automation, distributed architectures, and dynamically orchestrated assets.

Such a transformation also demands that the teams change to deployment models, infrastructure abstractions, and operational methods that are quite different as compared to the traditional application management methods.

The other critical problem will be the necessity of specialized skills and knowledge. Kubernetes is a complicated platform comprising numerous parts that are interconnected such as networking, storage, security, and observability systems. Companies need to invest in training and skill development to make sure that the engineering and operations departments are able to operate with Kubernetes clusters and resolve problems with distributed environments. Lack of proper expertise can lead to inefficiencies in the operations of the enterprises and high-risk levels within the system.

The collaboration between the development, operations, and security teams should also change in order to be adopted in an organization. Kubernetes architectures often accommodate the cloud-native development pattern that focuses on DevOps, continuous integration, and automated deployment pipelines. These practices can only be successfully implemented by aligning culture, having proper governance structures and working processes across teams. All these are organizational issues that need to be addressed as a way of ensuring that the adoption of Kubernetes contributes to long-term operational efficiency and enterprise scalability.

6.4.1 Skills Gap and Workforce Readiness

Kubernetes is an adopted platform in organizations due to its emergence as a common platform in deploying and administering containerized applications in production environment. It offers the capability to scale the applications and handle multifaceted workloads over distributed infrastructure. Nevertheless, after Kubernetes is implemented in the production setup, firms start to encounter its operational complexity. There are numerous new technologies, practices and models of operation that teams should be aware of when dealing with cloud-native infrastructure, instituted by Kubernetes.

Kubernetes environment is very complicated and introduces a big skills gap in most organizations. Kubernetes clusters can only be run by people who know a number of fields, such as container technologies, distributed systems, networking, storage, security and automation. This has meant that engineers tasked with the management of Kubernetes environments must have a wide-dispersed skillset in terms of technical abilities that is not necessarily encompassed in the traditional infrastructure management occupation.

The shortage of internal knowledge has proven to be one of the most commonly mentioned obstacles in the implementation of Kubernetes. According to industry reports, a significant proportion of the organizations note the shortage of skilled professionals as a significant impediment to the use of Kubernetes and cloud-native technologies. The increasing demand of Kubernetes skills has driven stiff competition in the job market whereby organizations face a challenge of hiring an engineer who has hands-on skills in the operational processes of Kubernetes platforms.

Besides recruitment issues, challenges have also been experienced by organizations in retaining talented Kubernetes engineers. Experts in Kubernetes and cloud-native technologies are in high demand in all spheres, which frequently results in high remuneration requirements and a tendency to change their workplace. This further puts a strain on organizations that are trying to achieve stable teams that can handle complex Kubernetes infrastructures.

To solve these problems, numerous companies invest in workforce development and training programs to enhance cloud-native engineering team competence. Training courses, certification routes, and knowledge sharing activities on the inside can assist groups to acquire the expertise necessary to run Kubernetes environments successfully. Organizations can enhance Kubernetes platforms management and accelerate long-term cloud-native adoption by making their workforce more readiness and developing internal capabilities.

6.4.2 Cultural and Operational Transformation

Much has been written about the technical features and benefits of Kubernetes. Technical advantages, however, are only part of the reason to migrate to Kubernetes. Cultural change is also an important aspect of Kubernetes adoption. In several ways, Kubernetes can help optimize how IT teams and developers are organized, regardless of their technology stacks or the types of organizations they work in. In turn, Kubernetes can improve how technical teams collaborate with each other and respond to business needs.

- **Why Culture Matters**

For technical personnel, it is easy to focus mainly on the technology used within an organization without considering the culture that shapes how that technology is used. In reality, technology and culture go hand-in-hand. Even the best technology stack will not deliver significant value if teams lack the cultural practices that allow them to use it effectively. Numerous prosperous technology companies have also realized the need to establish good cultures that foster responsibility, openness and constant improvement.

- **Automation**

Kubernetes promotes the culture of automation. Kubernetes offers automation which is an important aspect as it replaces manual work which used to be necessitated due to the need to deploy an application or migrate servers with automated processes. Kubernetes allows teams to embrace automation as a common practice in their daily operations by simplifying the implementation of automation to applications that operate on other infrastructures.

- **Scalability**

Another principle that Kubernetes assists organizations in embracing better is scalability. Conventional systems also tend to be poorly scalable since any modification in infrastructure facilities or application deployment involves manual administration. Kubernetes enables clusters and workloads to scale more simply and facilitates systems to expand with a limited number of nodes or workloads to much larger ones with little or no human intervention.

- **Transparency**

Kubernetes facilitates visibility in technical teams. It is an open-source platform with workloads being configured in standard formats in YAML configuration files. Due to the consistency and accessibility of these configurations, engineers can see and comprehend Kubernetes resources in the presence of other groups using the same resources. This mutual visibility minimizes the existence of silos in operations and also enhances team communication.

- **Standardization and Centralization.**

Centralization and standardization of workload management also become possible with the use of Kubernetes in an organization. The resources of Kubernetes can be controlled with the help of centralized repositories, like version control systems, and the same configuration practices can be used to make sure that deployments are made under the same operational standards. This assists the organizations to evade the scattered information and the inconsistent working methods.

- **Collaboration**

These traits are towards better teamwork. Kubernetes supports better interaction not only between developers and operations teams but also between IT teams and other parts of the organization. Because of the flexibility, transparency, and standardized management practices it enables, Kubernetes allows technical teams to respond more quickly to changing business requirements.

6.4.3 Tooling Complexity and Platform Standardization

Organizations face one of the most significant adversities when starting their Kubernetes adoption, which is the complexity of the cloud-native tooling ecosystem. The core orchestration platform is offered by Kubernetes, although in most cases, numerous additional tools used in networking, monitoring, logging, security, service meshes, and continuous integration and deployment pipelines are needed to run production workloads. Consequently, companies have to cope with many supporting technologies to successfully run Kubernetes environments.

Kubernetes ecosystem has grown at a very high rate, as now hundreds of open-source tools are available which can tackle various operational needs. On the one hand, this ecosystem offers flexibility and innovation; however, it is equally associated with challenges of choice and integration of tools. Most organizations are faced with the challenge of identifying what tools they need to incorporate into their infrastructure stack, and the way such tools are to be configured to interact with others. Kubernetes platforms in certain settings are based on various discrete tools in observability, CI/CD, security, and networking capabilities.

The fragmentation of tools may pose operational challenges like compatibility, complexity in configuration and may require more efforts in troubleshooting. It can also be common to use numerous independent tools and there needs to be further integration done to secure interoperability among various aspects of the platform. With Kubernetes environments growing to be multi-cluster and multi-cloud environments, there is an increased complexity in managing these inter-connected tools and can bring operational risks unless well-coordinated.

Platform standardization is what organizations pay attention to to overcome all these issues as the Kubernetes adoption strategy. Standardization assists in the mitigation of the complexity of handling various tools and infrastructure elements. Platform teams often provide uniform toolchains, deployment patterns, and practice configurations in order to provide uniformity between settings. This makes the management of clusters easier, more reliable, and allows development teams to roll out applications more effectively.

Moreover, platform engineering practices are widely used in many organizations to cope with the complexity of Kubernetes tooling. Platform Teams are teams within dedicated platforms that create standardized environments and automated workflows and pre-configured infrastructure components. Offering a stable platform layer, organizations are able to simplify operations and still have reliable and scalable Kubernetes environments.

6.4.4 Change Management and Organizational Alignment

Implementing Kubernetes and other cloud-native technologies can be a very change-intensive endeavour within an organization. The shift between the environment of traditional infrastructure to Kubernetes-based ones impacts the workflow, the organisational hierarchy, and the duties of work. With the shift towards containerized and automated infrastructure management, organizations need to change their current processes and organize changes among numerous teams and departments. In the absence of a proper change management, Kubernetes will cause operational inefficiency and delays in implementation.

Resistance to new technologies and practices is one of the biggest challenges during this change. In most organizations, the existing process of operations is long established and is based on a traditional infrastructure management. Implementation of Kubernetes comes with novel ideas like containerization, automation deployment and management of distributed systems. Such changes can mean that teams might need to alter the existing workflows and learn new working practices which can be slow to adopt unless organizations provide enough guidance, training and support.

The adoption of Kubernetes also demands alignment of the leadership and engineering teams with the operational units to achieve success. The leadership of the organization is significant in the definition of strategic objectives of the Kubernetes adoption and informing different teams about the anticipated benefits. By presenting objectives and responsibilities clearly to the leadership, development, operations, and security teams will be able to work together more efficiently. Absence of strategic direction can have the effect of fragmenting Kubernetes efforts and making them hard to manage in an organization-wide context.

The other factor of organizational alignment that is significant is the creation of collaborative working models amongst various teams. The Kubernetes environment usually involves close collaboration between the development team, operations teams, security experts, and platform engineers. These teams are required to collaborate to maintain infrastructure, provide applications, system performance and security policies. Interfunctional cooperation assists organizations in lessening operational silos and allows the team to administer Kubernetes environments in a better and more efficient manner.

Successful Kubernetes adoption thus needs proper change management and alignment of an organization. By providing a defined strategic direction, the necessity to support cultural change, and the possibility to encourage teamwork, organizations can ensure that Kubernetes projects align with their overall business objectives and contribute to the improved implementation of a cloud-native change.

Multiple-Choice Questions (MCQs)

1. **What is a key characteristic of a hybrid Kubernetes deployment model?**

   A) It runs only in a private data center
   B) It combines on-premises and cloud environments
   C) It avoids containerization
   D) It supports only monolithic applications

2. **Which of the following is a common reason organization choose on-premises Kubernetes deployments?**

   A) Unlimited public internet bandwidth
   B) Lower governance requirements
   C) Data residency, control, and regulatory needs
   D) No need for infrastructure management

3. **Which deployment model provides the greatest elasticity for Kubernetes workloads?**

   A) Bare-metal only
   B) Public cloud
   C) Air-gapped on-premises cluster
   D) Local virtual machine

4. **Which migration pattern is generally considered a practical first step for enterprise Kubernetes adoption?**

   A) Migrating every legacy workload at once
   B) Starting with stateless applications
   C) Replacing all databases immediately
   D) Disabling CI/CD pipelines

5. **Which of the following is considered an anti-pattern during Kubernetes migration?**

   A) Incremental modernization
   B) Pilot testing workloads

C) Lifting and shifting without redesign considerations
D) Establishing observability early

6. **What is the main purpose of governance in enterprise Kubernetes environments?**

A) To increase pod restart frequency
B) To enforce policies, standards, and operational control
C) To eliminate the need for security
D) To reduce cluster networking complexity only

7. **Which of the following is most closely related to compliance in Kubernetes environments?**

A) Horizontal Pod Autoscaler
B) Audit logging and access control
C) ReplicaSets
D) Service discovery only

8. **Which organizational challenge often slows Kubernetes adoption in enterprises?**

A) Too little need for automation
B) Lack of change management and skill development
C) Excessively simple application architectures
D) Reduced collaboration between teams

9. **In enterprise Kubernetes adoption, what is the role of platform engineering teams?**

A) To remove all application ownership from developers
B) To provide standardized internal platforms and operational guardrails
C) To avoid automation tools
D) To replace governance policies with manual processes

10. Which of the following best describes a successful enterprise Kubernetes adoption strategy?

A) Rapid deployment without policy planning
B) Centralized control with no developer enablement
C) Balanced focus on technology, people, and process
D) Avoiding cloud-native practices entirely

Answer

1	2	3	4	5	6	7	8	9	10
B	C	B	B	C	B	B	B	B	C

Chapter 7

The Future Of Kubernetes

7.1 Kubernetes and WebAssembly (WASM)

Kubernetes has become the most popular orchestration system of containerized workloads in cloud-native systems. As the application architectures keep on changing, there are new technologies that are materializing to supplement and enhance the functionality of container-based platforms. WebAssembly (WASM) is one of the most prospective advancements in the field: it is a lightweight runtime technology, which allows applications to be executed effectively in various environments. Combining WebAssembly and Kubernetes is a significant move in the future of cloud-native infrastructure.

Originally, WebAssembly was to be used to allow high-performance applications in web browsers, but in recent years it has greatly increased its functionality. Recent WebAssembly runtimes enable applications to execute safely and efficiently out of the browser, which makes WASM an appropriate fit to server-side workloads, edge computing and distributed cloud platforms. Due to its lightweight execution model and robust security isolation, WebAssembly is even considered a potential complement (or even a replacement) to the conventional container-based workloads.

WebAssembly and KubeIntegration allows organizations to operate WASM workloads and containerized applications on the same orchestration platform. This enables Kubernetes to handle more application runtimes and keep deployment, scaling, and operational management practices unchanged. WebAssembly workloads generally have a lower resource utilization and lower startup time than containers, which makes them especially appealing to microservices, serverless systems, and edge computing networks.

With the ongoing development of cloud-native ecosystems, numerous organizations and open-source communities are looking at ways in which WebAssembly can improve Kubernetes platforms. A number of new frameworks and runtime systems are being used to ensure that Kubernetes clusters can run WASM-based workloads, which open up new application portability, security, and performance optimization possibilities. These advancements indicate that WebAssembly can be an essential part of the future of the Kubernetes-based infrastructure.

7.1.1 Fundamentals of WebAssembly in Cloud-Native Environments

The browser was the original purpose for which WebAssembly was developed. But like Java and JavaScript before it, it gained popularity both on the server and at the edge as the community supported it, particularly through standardisation and toolchain development. WebAssembly was acknowledged as a significant programming technique in 2021 when it was given the ACM SIGPLAN Programming Languages Software Award.

Since many computing resources are abstracted into the cloud in the era of cloud-native computing, the distinction between hardware and software has grown more hazy. Microservices, messaging queues, data streams, and serverless tasks have all grown quickly as a result. These parts are frequently created by many developers and might potentially be unreliable, yet they must interact safely and efficiently within distributed systems. Traditional approaches for isolating software components, such as network-based APIs or container technologies like Docker, can introduce performance overhead and operational complexity.

For cloud-native software components, WebAssembly has become a high-performance, cross-platform, polyglot software sandbox. WebAssembly runtimes are compatible with a variety of host environments and programming languages, allowing applications to run consistently across different systems. Because of its lightweight execution model and strong sandboxing capabilities, WebAssembly provides a secure and efficient runtime environment for modern distributed applications. WebAssembly modules can be incorporated into data streaming frameworks or controlled and coordinated by container platforms.

In addition to hosting a number of related projects and efforts, the "Cloud Native Computing Foundation" (CNCF) actively promotes WebAssembly development and acceptance in cloud-native infrastructure.

- **WasmEdge** is a feature-rich WebAssembly runtime designed with cloud and edge computing applications in mind.
- **WasmCloud** is a WebAssembly host runtime based on actors that makes creating distributed WebAssembly apps easier.
- **Krustlet** is a kubelet implementation that allows Kubernetes nodes to run WebAssembly workloads directly, enabling WebAssembly programs to be scheduled as Kubernetes workloads.
- **Kubernetes**, as a container orchestration platform, can manage WebAssembly runtimes and orchestrate WebAssembly workloads alongside traditional containerized applications.
- **KubeEdge** is a runtime management and orchestration framework for edge computing that works with WebAssembly

runtimes to support applications on edge devices.

- **CRI-O** is an OCI-compliant container runtime that has been extended to support WebAssembly applications through integration with WebAssembly runtimes.
- **Envoy** uses WebAssembly to enable service mesh proxies' dynamic extensions, allowing developers to extend proxy functionality through WebAssembly modules.

The developments above underscore how WebAssembly is gaining relevance as a runtime technology in cloud-native ecosystems to enable its use in creating secure, portable and efficient execution of distributed applications in both cloud and edge execution.

7.1.2 WASM Workloads Kubernetes Integration.

With the introduction of WebAssembly (WASM), a safer and more portable means of running code in diverse contexts, application development and deployment has become possible with a wider range of options. In combination with Kubernetes, Wasm allows new methods of building, deploying, and managing applications in containerized environments. WebAssembly modules can run alongside traditional container workloads, allowing Kubernetes clusters to support lightweight and portable execution environments.

Understanding WebAssembly in the Context of Kubernetes

WebAssembly is a platform-neutral, fast, and safe binary instruction format of stack-based virtual machines. Wasm can be deployed under Kubernetes because of these features environments where applications must run across diverse infrastructure platforms.

- **Portability:** Any platform that supports a WebAssembly runtime can run Wasm modules. Applications packaged as Wasm modules can therefore be moved between development, testing, and production environments within Kubernetes without significant modifications caused by differences in underlying infrastructure.

- **Security:** WebAssembly executes in a sandboxed environment, restricting access to host system resources. This isolation is valuable in Kubernetes environments where minimizing the attack surface and preventing malicious code from affecting the host system or other workloads is a priority.

Real-World Applications of WASM in Kubernetes

WebAssembly is increasingly being used to support real-world workloads within Kubernetes environments.

1. **Krustlet:** Krustlet acts as a kubelet implementation that orchestrates WebAssembly modules instead of containers. It enables Kubernetes to schedule and manage Wasm workloads. Wasm modules can be used to execute lightweight programs like data transformation jobs with minimal resource usage and shorter startup times.
2. **Envoy Proxy Custom Filters:** Service meshes such as Istio use Envoy proxies that can support WebAssembly extensions. Wasm modules can be used to implement custom filters in the service mesh data plane. This enables dynamic customization of networking behaviour, such as enforcing security policies or implementing advanced routing logic without restarting or recompiling proxy services.
3. **SuborbitalAtmo:** SuborbitalAtmo orchestrates server-side logic using WebAssembly modules and declarative configurations. In Kubernetes environments, applications can be composed of multiple Wasm modules that interact with each other to deliver application services such as authentication, data processing, and backend integrations.
4. **Serverless Functions with WASM:** The lightweight nature of WebAssembly makes it suitable for serverless computing within Kubernetes clusters. Platforms such as OpenFaaS or Kubeless

can run serverless functions compiled into Wasm modules. These functions benefit from faster startup times and reduced resource overhead compared to traditional container-based functions.

5. **WasmEdge Runtime:** WasmEdge is a lightweight and high-performance runtime designed for WebAssembly workloads in cloud-native environments. In Kubernetes clusters, WasmEdge enables applications to execute WebAssembly modules at near-native speed. It can support scenarios such as IoT device management where multiple device interactions are handled through lightweight WebAssembly modules.

Challenges and Considerations with WASM in Kubernetes

When combining Kubernetes and WebAssembly provides several advantages, organizations must address a number of challenges.

1. **Runtime Environment Compatibility:** Although Wasm is designed to be platform independent, differences between WebAssembly runtimes such as Wasmtime, Wasmer, and WasmEdge can lead to variations in application behavior. Applications must therefore be tested across multiple runtimes to ensure consistent performance.
2. **Performance Considerations:** WebAssembly aims to deliver near-native performance, but performance can still be influenced by the abstraction layers used in different runtime environments. The benchmarking is required to make sure that WebAssembly workloads can run efficiently in Kubernetes clusters.
3. **ToolingandEcosystemMaturity**:TheKubernetesWebAssembly ecosystem is immature. The debugging, monitoring, and development tools are not yet mature in comparison to the ones that are offered to container-based environment, which can pose a challenge to large-scale implementation.
4. **Security Considerations**: WebAssembly offers strong sandboxing, but still, security requires the runtimes and modules to be configured appropriately. Networking and encryption should

also be used in ensuring that various modules communicate with external services.

5. **Operational Complexity**: The addition of WebAssembly workloads and container workloads adds further complexity to their operation. The teams need to be taught how to utilize new tools and workflows to handle the lifecycle of WebAssembly modules in Kubernetes.
6. **Integration with Existing Systems:** WebAssembly to be integrated in a Kubernetes configuration that now relies heavily on containers needs careful consideration, especially on issues like networking, service discovery, and workload-to-workload data exchange.
7. **Developer Adoption:** To become successful, WebAssembly should be heavily adopted by the developer community and WebAssembly applications must have libraries, frameworks, and tools that make their creation and implementation easier with Kubernetes.

7.1.3 Benefits of WASM for Kubernetes Platforms

WebAssembly has several interesting benefits when used in Kubernetes when compared to the traditional containers.

- **Fast**: In comparison with traditional containers, Wasm modules typically take milliseconds to launch. This low startup time is relevant in workloads with low startup time needs, including serverless functions and event-driven applications.
- **Lightweight:** Wasm modules consume less CPU and memory power and occupy less storage space than container images. Due to this, Kubernetes clusters are able to process bigger loads, and to utilize their resources effectively.
- **Secure:** Wasm modules are isolated along with the host operating

system, and run in a strict sandbox. This isolation reduces the effects of bad or flawed code in Kubernetes clusters and reduces potential security weaknesses.

- **Portable:** Wasm modules can be used with a wide range of CPU architectures and systems. Due to its portability, multiple container images of different operating systems and hardware environments would not need to be maintained.

The development of cloud-native computing is also coming to incorporate WebAssembly. Being the most popular container orchestration platform, Kubernetes keeps changing to utilize the potential of WebAssembly.

Kernel workloads on Kubernetes require two components to execute Wasm workloads.

Worker's node need a WebAssembly runtime environment bootstrapped with a Wasm runtime. This setup may be achieved by using lower-level runtimes with WebAssembly support such as crun and youki in combination with high-level container runtimes, such as containerd and CRI-O.

Nodes with a WebAssembly runtime are assigned to Runtime Class objects: objects allow Kubernetes to schedule workloads to specific nodes based on the runtime environment they support. In clusters where some nodes support WebAssembly runtimes and others support standard container runtimes, Runtime Class can be used to ensure that Wasm workloads are scheduled only on nodes that provide the appropriate runtime.

Additional benefits of using WebAssembly with Kubernetes include the following.

- **Performance:** Wasm applications can run at near-native speed, start faster than many containerized workloads, and operate within secure runtime environments.
- **Packaging:** Using container images as a packaging mechanism allows WebAssembly applications to integrate with existing CI/CD pipelines and deployment workflows.

- **Ecosystem:** By leveraging the Kubernetes ecosystem, WebAssembly workloads can benefit from the wide range of tools and services already designed to operate within Kubernetes environments.

7.1.4 Challenges and Future Potential of WASM in Kubernetes

Wasm also has some of the management issues that are presented by conventional containers. One or two Wasm modules can be easily loaded into a browser, but managing hundreds or thousands of back-end Wasm modules on the enterprise servers may be significantly harder. Hence, more modules have to be orchestrated and managed bigger. Though Wasm does not have a native orchestration platform, Kubernetes may be used in a Wasm environment.

In order to run Wasm modules in Kubernetes, the low-level runtime, as well as shim connecting the low-level runtime to the containerd management runtime, must be replaced. Among the most used shim replacements is the so-called runwasi that may be placed between containerd and low-level Wasm runtimes. Wasm runtimes also have a number of Wasmtime and WasmEdge.

Wasm modules can be loaded once configured as an alternative to containers. This substitution is effective since the shims, runtimes, workloads are mostly irrelevant to Kubernetes which scheduling tasks do not differentiate OCI-compliant containers and Wasm workloads.

Although the Wasm applications can be supported and scaled with the help of Kubernetes as a platform to organize applications, Wasm is not meant to substitute Docker containers. Kubernetes has the ability to scale between containers and Wasm workloads simultaneously to be more flexible in application design and deployment.

Wasm in Kubernetes has a number of benefits, such as lightweight and portable code, high-performance performance of complicated apps, simple integration of Wasm modules with Kubernetes, and an expanding ecosystem of Wasm runtimes. Moreover, Kubernetes does not need significant adjustments and can still be used to sustain the traditional container workloads as well as Wasm applications.

Nonetheless, the deployment of Wasm workloads on Kubernetes is accompanied by a number of difficulties as well. This also incurs extra learning of developers and operations teams as new runtimes, tools, and workflows are to be learned. The high count of Wasm runtimes may have different purposes, maturity, and vendor backing, which may make it difficult to pick and deal with runtimes.

The second problem is that no additional tools are needed to compile and test Wasm modules, and this factor could make CI/CD pipelines more complex. Moreover, the stability of the Wasm workloads in Kubernetes settings is under development. Most of the implementations are thought to be experimental and their stability and performance might not yet be good enough to be deployed to large scale production.

Even with these problems, there is currently an effort to better integrate Wasm into the Kubernetes ecosystem. Projects like Kwasm are also making Kubernetes coordinate and manage Wasm-based applications, enabling developers to take advantage of Kubernetes functionality like declarative configuration and automatic scaling and take advantage of the performance and security benefits of Wasm.

Wasm and Docker do not exclude each other in technology. Wasm modules may be built and served in Docker containers and it is possible to use the existing Docker ecosystem to distribute and manage them.

A supportive relationship between Wasm, Docker and Kubernetes is likely to occur in the future. WebAssembly has the ability to improve the portability, performance, and security of containerized applications and Kubernetes and Docker still offer the infrastructure needed to create, deploy, and maintain applications at scale. The future of the cloud-native application development is likely to be defined by more and more interaction of these technologies as the Wasm ecosystem continues to mature and get more adoption.

7.2 Serverless and event-driven convergence

Serverless computing and event-driven applications are entering the realm of the modern cloud-native system. With the trend of organizations moving towards microservices and distributed applications, there is a desire to have platforms where automatic response to events, dynamically scaled and reduced complexity in operations are supported. Kubernetes, a prominent container orchestration system, is changing, becoming capable of these features, by incorporating serverless systems and event-driven architectures into the ecosystem.

Serverless computing is a computing model that enables a developer to write application code and avoids taking care of the underlying infrastructure. Under this model functions or services are only implemented when an event triggers them, like an HTTP request, database update, or a queue message. It is a more efficient way to use resources since only when needed, compute resources are used, and the auto-scaling capability allows automated scaling of resources and lowers the overhead of operation.

Event-driven architecture is also complementary to the serverless model because it allows the system to respond to events raised by different event sources such as user interactions, application processes and external services. Events are stimuli that cause certain functionalities or workflows to be started enabling applications to asynchronously process tasks and react swiftly to the changes in the system state. The architecture is also especially applicable to cloud architecture where workloads can vary drastically.

The Kubernetes ecosystem includes Knative, Kubeless, and OpenFaaS as platforms which can be used to implement serverless and event-driven workloads. These platforms expand Kubernetes functionalities through function execution, auto scaling and routing of events. The convergence of serverless computing and event-driven architecture in Kubernetes is shaping the future of cloud-native application development by enabling highly scalable, responsive, and efficient systems.

7.2.1 Serverless Computing in Kubernetes

The advantages of serverless architecture, like autoscaling and on-demand execution, are combined with Kubernetes's container orchestration capabilities in serverless functions.

Applications or functions in a serverless paradigm only execute when they are triggered, automatically scaling up and down to meet demand without human intervention. Kubernetes is a powerful platform for serverless operations because it offers the infrastructure layer that scales and maintains containerised workloads.

Serverless applications can operate in a regulated and consistent environment by utilising Kubernetes, which uses containers to segregate dependencies and services. This method works well in multi-cloud and hybrid situations, as Kubernetes clusters provide a single platform for serverless function deployment and scalability.

Benefits of serverless on Kubernetes

There are several benefits to serverless deployment on Kubernetes, such as:

- **Scalability and resource efficiency:** Kubernetes' serverless services automatically scale in response to demand, cutting down on idle resources and increasing cost effectiveness. The "Horizontal Pod Autoscaler" (HPA) in Kubernetes makes ensuring that workloads grow or shrink as necessary, maximizing resource utilization.
- **Unified management between environments:** Kubernetes enables organisations to use serverless functions in on-prem, cloud, and hybrid environments. Besides simplifying the operations, this integration provides a standard framework on

how to roll out the applications and manage them.

- **Language and operation time flexibility:** Serverless solutions based on Kubernetes can execute functions in any language, ready to use as container images, unlike traditional serverless systems that may have restricted the languages and run times. This flexibility is useful to developers who deal with multiple languages and frameworks.
- **Improved observability and debugging:** Kubernetes provides metrics of the performance of functions, latencies, and resource usage and is compatible with monitoring and logging systems (Prometheus and Grafana). Its observability makes performance adjustment and troubleshooting easier.
- **Pursuant to Kubernetes ecosystem**: Organization will have the opportunity to deploy Kubernetes-native tools and services such as networking, security controls and service meshes and run serverless workloads on the platform. Such integration offers a greater control over application behavior and security in complex situations.
- **Less vendor lock-in:** Kubernetes serverless systems can work with any Kubernetes distribution, and are often free open source. This reduces dependence on one cloud provider, providing business with greater flexibility to deploy their workloads and where to do their work, and avoiding vendor lock-in.

The serverless architecture with Kubernetes.

Kubernetes Serverless architecture works by executing functions or applications, which respond to events and do not involve a developer to control the underlying infrastructure at all. Kubernetes serves as the orchestration layer, managing these functions as containerized workloads, and handling aspects like scheduling, scaling, and failover:

- **Event-driven execution:** Functions in serverless Kubernetes settings are triggered by events, such as database updates, queue messages, or HTTP requests. Event sources offer the events that start function execution by connecting to the serverless platform via messaging protocols or APIs. Developers can specify event triggers for their functions using serverless frameworks such as Knative Eventing or OpenFaaS.

- **Autoscaling and resource management:** Kubernetes' Horizontal Pod Autoscaler (HPA) and other scaling technologies are used by serverless frameworks to scale functions according to demand. Kubernetes quickly sets up containers to handle incoming requests when a function is activated, scaling up as demand rises and down when it falls. This elasticity ensures that the computational resources are not consumed to unnecessary levels and minimizes costs.
- **Isolation and lifecycle management**: Each serverless function runs within a container, as well as in order to offer isolation among functions as well as to avoid interference of dependencies and runtime environments. Kubernetes controls the lifecycle of these containers and also starts, reinstates and stops them when necessary. Isolation and lifecycle management are needed to ensure the security and reliability of large or multi-tenant applications.
- **Observability and control:** Kubernetes make it easier to understand the performance of functions, the utilization of resources, and latency of their execution by integrating with logging and monitoring tools such as as Prometheus and Grafana. These insights can help administrators to optimize serverless processes by identifying bottlenecks, fixing issues and tuning up the function setups.

7.2.2 Event-Driven Architecture in Kubernetes

Event-Driven Architecture (EDA) is a design paradigm whereby the events control the way a system behaves. Events can be a user action, a sensor output, or a message of another system. It is through the real-time responsiveness of the application to these events that dynamic and responsive interactions are possible in EDA.

Essential Elements of EDA

- **Event Producers:** Event producers are the producers of events. These may be application, IoT devices or user interfaces. These producers make events every time something significant happens.
- **Routers for Events:** Event routers or brokers are those in charge of managing and directing events to the correct customers. They make communication between the producers and the customers easy since they make sure that the events are available at the right place. Examples are Amazon SNS and Apache Kafka.
- **Event Attendees:** The event consumers are the entities that respond to factors. Depending on the data of the event, they will be able to perform several tasks, such as sending a notification, modifying a database, or initiating another process.

Advantages of EDA

- **Disconnecting:** Decoupling of components simplifies the updating and maintenance of individual component of the system without the overall effect on the system. Having numerous advantages that enhance performance, scalability, and flexibility of modern systems, EDA has emerged as an essential design paradigm of the cloud-native development.
- **Flexibility and Scalability:** With the help of EDA, applications can handle many events in an asynchronous manner, enabling components to independently scale up and down due to demand. Kubernetes and other cloud-native offer a seamless autoscaling, where resources can be allocated and distributed dynamically as required. To this flexibility, applications can easily manage unpredictable demands without excessive provision of resources.
- **Modularity and Decoupling:** One of the greatest benefits of EDA is the decoupling of components. In an event-driven system,

both consumers and producers do not know the origin and source of the events respectively, nor do they know about the intended consumers and producers. Such loose coupling enhances maintainability and reduces chances of failure at system wide levels since individual components can be developed, deployed and upgraded separately.

- **Processing in Real Time:** EDA comes in handy when instant responses and processing of real time data are required. The ability of EDA to handle events in real-time and to act on them is beneficial when it comes to solutions such as a fraud detection system, IoT, and real-time analytics.
- **Fault Tolerance and Resilience:** Event driven systems can be designed to be very robust. Failure of any single component in the system does not impact the system because events are not concentrated in only one of the consumers. Cloud-native environments provide even greater resilience with high fault tolerance techniques.
- **Increased Reactivity:** Event and change response can be implemented in applications when they occur because of EDA and hence the user experience is more dynamic and responsive.

Better scalability, modularity, real-time processing, and resilience are only a few of the numerous features that EDA would offer to cloud-native development. With the help of EDA, developers can develop scalable systems that are responsive to complex real-time data processing tasks within the modern distributed environment. Challenges and Future Potential of Serverless and Event-Driven Convergence

Serverless computing and event-driven architectures are being written together in the modern cloud-native systems. In this architecture, programs are executed small programs in response to event such as user requests, API calls or messages sent by distributed systems. Serverless computing enables functions to be executed on an event basis and thus allows applications to automatically scale and perform efficiently without the developers having to take care of the underlying infrastructure.

Although these benefits exist, there are a few issues associated with deploying serverless and event-driven systems to large-scale systems. Among the major issues are cold start problem which causes delay as the platform loads a new execution environment and then executes a function. Such latency may impact on applications that demand immediate responses or applications with low latency.

The other area is observability and debugging on distributed serverless environments. According to serverless applications, a large number of short-lived functions are invoked based on various events and it is challenging to trace the execution between the system. Observability frameworks, centralized logging, and distributed tracing can thus be advanced tools used to monitor and debug.

There are also architectural challenges associated with events management systems which takes place in event driven systems. The systems should be careful in event generation, delivery and processing so as to rule out potential issues such as event overload, data inconsistency or event order loss. Distributed environments need proper event routing and error-handling mechanisms in order to be reliable.

Nevertheless, the integration of serverless computing with event-driven architecture is ongoing and is changing at a very high pace. Knatives are platforms like Knative that can be used to complement Kubernetes with serverless and event-driven features that ensure automatic scaling, event routing, and Microservice deployment on demand.

In the future, this convergence is likely to be a major part in the future of cloud-native application development. Event-driven and serverless models allow highly scalable, cost-effective and real-time responsive systems. With the ongoing development of orchestration platforms, monitoring technologies, and event-processing technologies, the convergence of serverless and event-controlled architectures and Kubernetes will emerge as a major way of creating distributed and resilient applications.

7.3 Platform abstraction trends

As cloud-native technologies are still being advanced, it has become an issue of managing complex infrastructure environments within organizations. Kubernetes has become a potentially influential platform to coordinate containerized applications; however, its expanding ecosystem and complexity of operations may present a barrier to development teams engaging directly with the underlying infrastructure. The way forward to overcome this challenge is platform abstraction trends, which are aimed at providing simplified applications development, deployment, and management on Kubernetes.

Platform abstraction is the development of higher-level platforms or tools that expose little or nothing of the complexity of the underlying infrastructure yet exploit the capabilities of Kubernetes. Rather than connecting with low-level configuration details, developers have the opportunity to implement applications through standardized interfaces, automated workflows, and self-service platforms. With this type of approach, development teams treat infrastructure management with less seriousness and more attention on application logic.

The rise of platform engineering (organizations develop internal developer platforms (IDPs) on top of Kubernetes) is one of the most important processes that contributes to the abstraction of platforms. The environments offered through these platforms are preconfigured, have templates that can be reused, and automated deployment pipelines which simplify the application development and operation. Abstracting complexity of infrastructures, platform engineering assists organizations to boost the productivity of their developers, consistency between environments, and best practices.

Platform abstraction will play a bigger role in future cloud-native development as the Kubernetes ecosystem is more mature. Infrastructure management tools and frameworks that are easy to use and yet provide the flexibility and scalability required by large scale distributed systems are becoming a necessity to organizations that run such systems. The trends show that there is a transition to friendlier platforms that integrate automation, standardization, and abstraction to handle intricate Kubernetes settings effectively.

7.3.1 Concept of Platform Abstraction in Cloud-Native Systems

Effective cloud operations only begin with the implementation of a sound operating model. It talks about people and procedures, but what about technology? Organisations must adopt and use tools that are independent of cloud environments and providers in order to expand the operating model. These tools are a reaction to the cloud sprawl phenomena, which is the use of various cloud providers.

Cloud sprawl frequently results in a complexity wall when problems arise, apps malfunction, and expenses suddenly increase. Organisations should use abstraction to reduce complexity. Abstracted tooling allows the customer to concentrate on the broad picture by concealing details from them. Organisations can eliminate complexity barriers to innovation and lessen the technological redundancy of point products by selecting abstracted tools.

Ansible for configuration management, terraform for infrastructure provisioning, and Cloud-Native Application Protection Platforms (CNAPP) like Prisma Cloud, which works with all cloud service providers, are a few examples of abstracted solutions. Organisations should inventory their current cloud tools, find non-abstracted products that can be replaced, and adopt abstracted tools for their CI/CD, security, and configuration management requirements in order to minimize complexity.

The field of platform engineering focuses on creating and managing software development platforms that enable developer team's self-service and the infrastructure required to provision an application.

Developer self-service allows for the complete flow of development, testing, documentation, deployment, rollback, and other development operations. It came about as a result of the desire to get past the drawbacks of traditional software development, which was frequently marked by complicated infrastructures, separated teams, long cycles, and silos. Enhancing the developer experience (DevEx) and streamlining software delivery are the primary objectives of platform engineering.

Platform engineering frees developers to concentrate on code and business logic by simplifying the underlying infrastructure and procedures. The proliferation of tools and artefacts in the "everything as code" era, the growing complexity of infrastructure, the cloud computing era with various providers and vendors, and multi-cloud adoption all contributed to an increase in the cognitive load of developers. Another issue was the absence of design patterns.

As an internal provider, a platform engineering team provides a layer of abstraction that enables developers to work more autonomously and effectively. The "platform as a product" mentality, which views the platform as a product with internal developers as its clients, is the driving force behind this strategy. This task is centralized in platform engineering, which ensures the uniformity, scalability, and optimization across the company and is not done by individual development teams building and maintaining their own infrastructure and tools.

Platform engineering allows developers to perform more common tasks such as resource provisioning, deployment of applications, configuration management through self-service interfaces such as APIs, automation tools, and developer portals. Because of this abstraction, developers may work with standardized platforms while the platform itself handles the operational complexity and underlying infrastructure.

7.3.2 Platform Engineering and Internal Developer Platforms (IDPs)

The field of platform engineering is devoted to creating and managing software development platforms that give developer teams self-service, such as the infrastructure required to provision an application. Developer self-service can handle every step of the process, including development, testing, documentation, deployment, rollback, etc. It came about as a result of the desire to get past the drawbacks of traditional software development, which was frequently marked by complicated infrastructures, separated teams, long cycles, and silos. Optimizing software delivery and enhancing the developer experience (DevEx) are the primary objectives of platform engineering.

Platform engineering essentially aims to: Offer standardized tools and services Provide a collection of tools, services, and workflows that make it simple for developers to create, implement, and maintain their applications. IDEs, CLIs, project templates, code versioning, CI/CD pipelines, container orchestration tools, configuration management tools, and observability systems are a few examples of these technologies.

Reduce complexity: Developers can concentrate on code and business logic by abstracting the intricacy of the underlying infrastructure and activities. The proliferation of tools and artefacts in the "everything as code" era, the growing complexity of infrastructure, the cloud computing period with several providers and suppliers, and multi-cloud adoption all contributed to a rise in the cognitive load of developers. Another issue was the absence of design patterns.

Boost productivity by removing bottlenecks and repetitive procedures and speeding up the development and deployment cycle. This is accomplished by automating processes like configuration management, application deployment, and infrastructure provisioning.

Enhance security and governance by integrating security and compliance procedures into the platforms right away. Platform engineering aims at a more secure and compliant configuration, through the combination of security measures and governance policies.

Encourage cooperation: Encourage cooperation amongst the product, security, operations, and development teams. The platform serves as an interface that enables various teams to collaborate more effectively, see solutions, and identify what is required for the advancement of their job.

On top of infrastructure, an internal development platform (IDP) is a self-service layer that provides developers with a simplified interface to access the environments, tools, and services they require to create and deliver code. This covers deployment best practices, CI/CD pipeline orchestration, and infrastructure and access control provisioning.

Platforms offer automated self-service solutions that minimize complexity and eliminate any bottlenecks resulting from an excessive dependence on DevOps and third-party input. Consider it as a centralized hub that frees engineers to concentrate on creating code by removing the complexity of the tech stack.

IDPs are not the same as internal development portals, which are usually more concerned with expanding the capabilities of IDPs and exchanging expertise and documentation. IDPs go one step further by offering real operational capabilities, even though both seek to increase developer productivity.

Key features and components of internal developer platforms include:

- **Self-service access:** IDPs give developers on-demand access to tools and resources. With the help of this functionality, team members may manage services, deploy apps, and provision environments without waiting for assistance from the operations or IT teams.
- **Service catalog:** A service catalogue serves as an organization's central repository for all services, APIs, and resources that are available. It also provides information on the ownership and status of each service as well as usage guidelines.

- **CI/CD integrations:** Automated builds, testing, and deployments across development environments are made possible by integration with continuous integration and continuous deployment pipelines.
- **Security and compliance automation:** To make sure that code complies with company and industry standards, IDPs integrate automated security scans and compliance checks into development workflows.
- **Observability and monitoring tools:** Application performance, resource usage, and system health are all visible through the integration of monitoring and observability tools with internal developer platforms.
- **Collaboration and knowledge sharing:** Collaboration between development teams and other stakeholders is enhanced by shared dashboards, documentation, and communication connections.

7.3.3 Tools and Frameworks supporting Platform Abstraction

Modern platform abstraction relies on a combination of tools and frameworks that automate infrastructure management, standardize development workflows, and provide simplified interfaces for developers. The tools assist the platform teams in creating internal developer platforms and extract the complexity of the cloud infrastructure without sacrificing scalability or operational control.

- **Container Orchestration Using Kubernetes.**

Kubernetes is an open-source software used in managing, scaling and deploying containerized applications. Some of the tasks that Kubernetes can automate include as networking, security, scaling and container configuration. Kubernetes is a useful application package automation tool that contains a number of containers. It also enables developers to bundle and isolate container clusters to deploy simultaneously with a large number of machines. Kubernetes can automatically create containers and allocate them based on the needs of scalability and demand.

- **Cross plane Cross Kubernetes Infrastructure Management Cross plane.**

Cross plane helps organizations to develop and use control planes over Kubernetes. Cross plane can be used to coordinate infrastructure resources of various cloud providers using Kubernetes APIs. Cross plane is compatible with cloud-native tools because it has a similar base with Kubernetes and enables platform teams to operate infrastructure and services in a similar manner.

- **GitLab CI/CD Continuous Integration and Deployment.**

GitLab CI/CD is a software development tool using continuous methods such as "Continuous Integration" (CI), Continuous Delivery (CD) and Continuous Deployment. Applications are automatically created, tested, deployed and monitored. The development cycle must identify bugs and errors at an early stage to ensure that the code that is released to the production meets the required standards.

- **Argo CD Continuous Deployment.**

Argo CD is a Kuber-native continuous deployment solution that runs modern applications. Argo CD can be used by developers to deploy new code into Kubernetes resources. It offers automatic matching of application condition and declarative setup, placed in repositories, and web interfaces, command-line programs and role-based authorization of deployments across clusters.

- **Docker as a Containerization tool.**

Dockers could also be used to develop, test, deploy, run and manage applications in a containerized architecture using Docker, an open-source platform. Each container contains the libraries, configuration, dependencies and application code required to run the program. Containerization and micro services are used in platform engineering to enhance application development and deployment.

- **Terraform Infrastructure Provisioning.**

Infrastructure can be defined and operated in a team with Terraform, which is an open-source infrastructure-as-code tool, with configuration files. Terraform provides and manages cloud resources in AWS, Azure, Google Cloud, and Kubernetes by defining the how infrastructure is to be configured. This automation makes it simple to operate infrastructure and facilitates the consistent deployment of complex environments.

- **Port for Developer Portals**

Port has been chosen as a centralized infrastructure and application management interface. Using customizable dashboards, teams can focus on relevant KPIs, whereas integrations with other tools, including GitHub and Jira, can be used to unify infrastructure tools, services, and documentation. The developer portals ease in standardization of development process, and offer a central point of dealing with projects and documentation.

- **Datadog for Monitoring and Observability**

Datadog is a monitoring and analytics platform for cloud-scale applications that provides full-stack observability. It collects and visualizes metrics and logs across infrastructure, enabling teams to monitor application performance, detect anomalies, and troubleshoot issues. Its integrations with cloud services and development tools support real-time insights and operational visibility.

Together, these tools and frameworks support platform abstraction by automating infrastructure provisioning, standardizing deployment processes, enabling developer self-service platforms, and providing observability across cloud-native environments.

7.3.4 Impact of Platform abstraction on Cloud-Native Development

Cloud-native development is greatly influenced by platform abstraction because it makes management of infrastructure easier and software delivery processes become more efficient. Organizations can make distributed clouds environments less complex by adding standardized platforms and automation layers and allow their development teams to build applications instead of managing infrastructure elements.

Another great impact of platform abstraction is that it enhances developer productivity and developer experience. Internal developer platforms and platform engineering offer pre-fabricated tools and services as well as workflows which enable developers to deploy and manage applications without writing extensively about what goes behind the scenes. This facilitates cognitive load and allows developers to focus on features and innovations delivery.

Platform abstraction is also faster in delivering software and time to market. Infrastructure provisioning, deployment pipelines, workflows and other operational processes can be automated, allowing development teams to release applications and updates more reliably and with reduced pace. Organizations are able to streamline development cycles and increase the rate of deployment and also have consistency in environments with automated platforms.

The other notable impact is that it has brought more cooperation and consistency of development teams. Platform abstraction unites tools, services and workflows, and it creates one entity, which enables teams to collaborate more effectively. The standard processes can be applied in maintaining consistency in software development processes, reducing errors in configuration, and also, compliance with the company policies.

Platform abstraction is also the source of the increased scalability of cloud-native and operational efficiency. With the help of automation, container orchestration, and cloud-native infrastructure platforms, organizations are able to deal with large-scale distributed applications in a more successful way. The platforms offer a scalable base upon which cloud-native applications can be deployed, developed, and operated so that they can serve changing workloads and business needs.

In general, platform abstraction is an important factor in the context of contemporary cloud-native development as it enhances the productivity of the developers, speeds up the delivery of the software, improves collaboration and allows the management of the infrastructure at scale. With the ongoing development of cloud-native systems, platform abstraction is emerging as a fundamental way of managing intricate application environments, as well as handling the efficient application of software development practices.

7.4 Problems Kubernetes is not designed to solve

Kubernetes has emerged and is the standard system of container management and cloud-native application orchestration. It offers potent features of deploying, scaling and managing container workloads on distributed infrastructure. Kubernetes simplifies the work of complicated architectures of microservices through several features, including automated scheduling, self-healing, service discovery, and horizontal scaling.

Even with all its capabilities, Kubernetes is not the solution to all the issues connected with the software development, the infrastructure management, and the functioning of enterprises. It is particularly created to operate container applications and infrastructure necessary to execute them, as opposed to the entirety of application architecture, business logic, or organizational processes. These limitations are noteworthy to organizations considering Kubernetes as one of their technology stacks.

Most organizations start with the belief that Kubernetes can serve as a fully functional platform to all the operational and development problems. Nonetheless, Kubernetes is mainly concerned with orchestration and automation of infrastructure. Other areas of concern, including application design, data management, security governance, and organizational workflows, may also demand other tools, frameworks, or operating practices on top of Kubernetes.

Awareness of Kubernetes limits assists organizations to construct superior cloud-native systems. Through awareness of what Kubernetes is good at and the complementary technologies needed, teams may become able to construct more balanced systems that are a combination of container orchestration and more focused platforms to monitor, be secure, manage data, and build applications.

7.4.1 Application Architecture and Software Design Challenges

Kubernetes is created as a container orchestration platform, which automates the deployment, scaling and management of containerized applications. It offers infrastructure-level services like scheduling workloads, cluster state management, container distribution to nodes and efficient use of resources in distributed systems. Such features ensure Kubernetes is very efficient in the operation of large-scale systems that are containerized.

In any case, Kubernetes does not address issues associated with application architecture or software design. It controls containers and infrastructure resources but is not aware of the inner logic of application or how software pieces are organized. Problems involving application performance, code quality, system design need to be resolved during the development and architectural planning phases and not with Kubernetes orchestration.

Several common architectural challenges remain outside the scope of Kubernetes.

- **Poor application design**

Kubernetes is not able to patch bad applications. Inefficient algorithms, blocking code, memory leaks, or components that are tightly coupled are all problems that are rooted in the software design choices. Although the application may be scaled using the Kubernetes application to several containers, these weaknesses may still cause bottlenecks in the performance and stability of the system.

- **Microservice architecture complexity**

Recent cloud-native applications tend to have microservice architecture. Kubernetes is able to deploy, scale, and deal with microservices, but it does not dictate the design of these services and their interactions with other services. Developers and system architects need to make decisions regarding service boundaries, API design and patterns of communication.

- **Service communication and latency**

Applications developed using numerous distributed services tend to depend on network communication among objects. Badly implemented service interactions may lead to high call counts, high latencies, and restarting failures. Kubernetes is a networking infrastructure that does not optimize application-level communication patterns.

- **Software development lifecycle management**

Kubernetes lacks the entire software development lifecycle. Writing source code, application development, software testing, and maintaining CI/CD pipelines are developed using tooling that is not tied to Kubernetes and engineering processes. The platform is more related to the operation of containerized workloads and not the development or design of them.

To conclude, Kubernetes is a very useful tool with great potential to organize containers and coordinate infrastructural resources, but it should not substitute acceptable application architecture and quality software engineering. Properly designed apps, proper division of services, and effective patterns of communication are all crucial issues of developers and system architects.

7.4.2 Data Management and Stateful Workloads

The persistent data may be a problem to Kubernetes practitioners since it was initially created to run stateless workloads. Kubernetes is very dependent on declarative and volatile containers, where workers may be recreated on-demand to reach a desirable state. Nevertheless, persistent data cannot be restarted identically to application containers, and this further complicates the process of executing stateful applications.

Traditional container environment more or less assumes that applications are disposable entities and can be easily replaced in case of failure. Databases, messaging services, and other stateful services differ as they are based on data with a long lifespan that has to be available even when the underlying containers have been changed. This contrast between temporary containers and permanent data poses an inherent difficulty of using Kubernetes as a stateful workload.

Kubernetes tries to overcome such problems with the aid of multiple mechanisms including persistent volumes, persistent volume claims, and Stateful Sets. These features enable applications to persist data outside the container lifecycle so that data will still be available even when the pods have been restarted. Although the mechanisms allow stateful applications to be deployed on Kubernetes, they do not reduce the complexity of managing persistent data.

Separation of the application data and application configuration is another challenge of importance. Application configuration in Kubernetes is commonly contained in manifests, environment variables or configuration maps, and the data is contained in persistent volumes. The stateful applications thus need coordination between the underlying resources of storage and the configuration definition itself to manage, migrate or protect them.

Due to these reasons, stateful workloads on Kubernetes can easily demand the implementation of supplementary storage platforms, backup services, and operational habits. Although Kubernetes offers the platform on which the management of containers on a large scale is conducted, the maintenance of rational data management strategies is still the domain of secondary Kubernetes.

7.4.3 Security Governance and Organizational Policies

Kubernetes is based on a cloud-native architecture and draws on advice from the Cloud Native Computing Foundation (CNCF) about good practices for cloud-native information security. These practices guide organizations in securing Kubernetes clusters and the applications running on them.

Kubernetes provides several built-in security mechanisms, APIs, and policy controls that help organizations implement governance and enforce security policies across containerized environments. These mechanisms support the protection of infrastructure components, workloads, and sensitive data.

1. Kubernetes Security Mechanisms

Kubernetes includes several APIs and security controls, as well as ways to define policies that can form part of how organizations manage information security.

2. Control Plane Protection

A key security mechanism for any Kubernetes cluster is controlling access to the Kubernetes API. Kubernetes expects administrators to configure and use **TLS encryption** to provide data encryption in transit within the control plane and between the control plane and its clients.

Encryption at rest can also be enabled for the data stored within the Kubernetes control plane. This protection is separate from encryption used for application workloads and their stored data.

3. Secrets Management

The **Secret API** provides basic protection for configuration values that require confidentiality. Secrets allow sensitive information such as passwords, API keys, and tokens to be stored and managed securely within Kubernetes.

4. Workload Protection

Workload security in Kubernetes can be enforced through multiple mechanisms:

- **Pod Security Standards** help ensure that Pods and their containers are isolated appropriately.
- **Runtime Classes** allow administrators to define custom runtime isolation environments.
- **Network Policies** control network traffic between Pods or between Pods and external networks.

Organizations can also deploy additional security tools from the broader Kubernetes ecosystem to implement preventative or detective controls for Pods, containers, and container images.

5. Admission Control

Admission controllers are plugins that intercept Kubernetes API requests. These controllers can validate or modify requests before they are processed by the cluster.

Correct design of admission controllers will aid the enforcement of organizational policies and avoid misconfigurations besides maintaining compatibility with updates in Kubernetes version.

6. Auditing and Monitoring

Kubernetes has audit logging, which creates a chronology of what has been done in the cluster. Such logs do record operations made by users, applications communicating with the Kubernetes API, and even the control plane. Security monitoring, incident investigation and compliance reporting are necessary based on audit logs.

7. Policy Enforcement

The Kubernetes-native mechanisms that can be used to define security policies include:

- **Network Policy**, which provides declarative control over network packet filtering.
- **Validating Admission Policy**, which restricts changes made through the Kubernetes API.

Besides indigenous policies, external policy frameworks and ecosystem tools are available to organizations to implement governance regulations regarding the source code review, container image approval, networking, and API access control.

Multiple-Choice Questions (MCQs)

1. **What is one major reason WebAssembly (WASM) is gaining interest in Kubernetes environments?**

   A) It replaces all operating systems
   B) It enables lightweight, fast, and portable workloads
   C) It removes the need for networking
   D) It eliminates the need for orchestration

2. **How does WASM differ from traditional containers in Kubernetes?**

   A) WASM workloads are usually lighter and start faster
   B) WASM requires more resources than containers
   C) WASM cannot run in distributed systems
   D) WASM replaces Kubernetes completely

3. **What is the main goal of serverless and event-driven convergence with Kubernetes?**

   A) To increase manual infrastructure management
   B) To allow applications to respond automatically to events
   C) To remove scalability features
   D) To prevent automation in cloud-native systems

4. **Which of the following is a common use case for event-driven workloads in Kubernetes?**

   A) Static file storage only
   B) Triggering application functions when an event occurs
   C) Replacing all databases
   D) Removing CI/CD pipelines

5. **What does “platform abstraction” in Kubernetes mainly aim to achieve?**

   A) Expose more infrastructure complexity to developers
   B) Hide unnecessary operational complexity from application teams
   C) Remove automation from DevOps workflows
   D) Replace all cloud platforms with one vendor

6. **Which tool or concept is often associated with Kubernetes platform abstraction?**

   A) Internal Developer Platforms (IDPs)
   B) Manual shell scripting only
   C) Standalone desktop applications
   D) Spreadsheet-based deployment systems

7. **Which of the following is a problem Kubernetes is not designed to solve directly?**

   A) Container orchestration
   B) Service discovery
   C) Poor application architecture design
   D) Scaling workloads

8. **Why is Kubernetes not considered a complete solution for all enterprise IT problems?**

   A) Because it only works on laptops
   B) Because it focuses on orchestration, not every software or business challenge
   C) Because it cannot run in the cloud
   D) Because it does not support automation

9. **What is a likely future trend in Kubernetes adoption?**

   A) More abstraction layers to simplify developer experience
   B) Complete abandonment of automation
   C) Replacement of distributed systems with monolithic mainframes
   D) Elimination of observability tools

10. Which statement best describes the future direction of Kubernetes?

A) It will remain only a low-level infrastructure tool
B) It is evolving to support diverse runtimes, automation, and developer-friendly platforms
C) It will only be used for legacy applications
D) It will stop integrating with cloud-native technologies

Answer

1	2	3	4	5	6	7	8	9	10
B	A	B	B	A	A	C	B	A	B

References

Baran, E. (2024). Designing service discovery and load balancing in a microservices architecture. *Cerbos*. https://www.cerbos.dev/blog/service-discovery-load-balancing-microservices

Cloudflare. (2025). What is load balancing? | How load balancers work. *Cloudflare Color*. https://www.cloudflare.com/learning/performance/what-is-load-balancing/

Shah, N. (2025). What is Service Discovery? Complete guide [2026 Edition]. *Middleware*. https://middleware.io/blog/service-discovery/

About The Author

Siri Chava is a Cloud Architect and Platform Engineering specialist with a passion for designing resilient, scalable, and self-healing cloud ecosystems. Their journey into large-scale systems began with a broken Linux machine and a determination to understand how complex technologies work and fail. That early curiosity evolved into a career focused on architecting robust cloud-native platforms that reduce operational toil and improve reliability.

Siri has led large-scale migrations to Amazon EKS and implemented advanced scaling solutions such as Karpenter, enabling efficient, automated infrastructure management. Their work emphasizes declarative infrastructure, streamlined CI/CD pipelines, and platform strategies that transform fragmented environments into unified, production-ready systems.

With a strong systems-thinking mindset, Siri bridges the gap between low-level technical automation and high-level business strategy. Beyond cloud architecture, they are interested in systems philosophy, emerging technologies, and the broader patterns that shape modern engineering and innovation.

www.ingramcontent.com/pod-product-compliance
Lightning Source LLC
LaVergne TN
LVHW022156200926
848481LV00006B/1760
9798904796716